Pro-Life Democrat

Pro-Life Democrat

50 Brief Insights

an apologia

by John Cavanaugh-O'Keefe

ISBN: 9798587720237

Dedication

To Gerry and Cathy Roth
– loving, persistent, fearless –

*Thanks for decades
of respectful argument*

Contents

Introduction

I'm a bridge. I may do it well, or I may do it poorly – but I'm a bridge. I'm a bridge between the left and the right of a church that should be united. That is, I am a social justice advocate and I am a pro-lifer, and so I am a bridge between the two. I try, consciously and deliberately, to be a visible and useful bridge, albeit flawed.

This is not history, nor biography, nor an argument. It's an apologia: I try to explain myself.

This is not an explanation offered to fellow Democrats about why I'm a pro-lifer; I've done that elsewhere. (See, for example, *Emmanuel, Solidarity: God's Act, Our Response*.) This is instead addressed to fellow pro-lifers, explaining why I'm a Democrat.

A large number of my old friends think I'm a traitor. I've had two friends get so mad when they denounced my treachery that they foamed at the mouth, with several teaspoonsful of fluffy white spit leaking out the corners of their mouths, oozing down and dripping off their chins. It was an interesting experience – a little uncomfortable but still fascinating. I had heard of this thing before and seen it in comedies; but was it real, or just a joke? It's real! There it was, right in front of me! Wow! It's good that they were shouting, or I would have been completely distracted by the visual presentation, and lost track of what they were saying.

What bubbled out was that I'm a traitor to the pro-life movement. Hm. I've been speaking up for the unborn since 1972, getting on towards half a century. If I'm a traitor, that's actually a pretty impressive bit of traiting. But I plead innocent.

The evidence against me is generally pretty clear: I'm a Democrat. There are other details: I'm pro-union, and I support civil rights, and I like to find common ground, and I prize civility. But the key charge against me is simple: I'm a Democrat. And that's a fact.

I wonder if we can talk about this. I'm not sure we can: I was impressed by the foam! But I'd like to try.

I think of myself as a pro-lifer. In fact, I think of myself as a pro-life leader (albeit past my prime – ah, well). Even more, I think I see a way forward when most of the pro-life leaders whom I know – many of them friends over the past decades – are stuck, mired, lost – setting their sights lower and lower each year.

I think the pro-life movement should grow, not shrink. When pro-lifers denounce Democrats and liberals and lefties and such, that's a lot of people to lose, and it doesn't help save babies. This angry division does have some effects: (1) it strengthens Planned Parenthood, and (2) it helps the Republican Party; it's good for them. But how can anyone ever think that this determination to divide and reject is good for the pro-life movement, better for the unborn?

So let me try to shift the conversation a bit. Let me give you 50 short insights into my thinking, 50 anecdotes or observations. Each of them should stand on its own, complete and independent, answering the question at least partially: "Why are you a Democrat?" Added together, I think they offer a clear and convincing argument, but let's go through them one small bite at a time.

Part I: Who Needs Strategy?

Strategy: a plan of action designed to achieve an overarching goal
Tactics: specific steps designed to achieve specific goals, usually interim goals
Tactics without strategy is just noise before defeat.

The bull snorted. "Look at that fool with his red flag! Doesn't he know what I can do? I'm gonna rip everything into tiny bits!" The cow watched and chewed some more. This looked familiar, but it didn't look good.

The pro-life movement is operating without a coherent strategy. Most pro-life leaders are fixated on an interim goal, reversing Roe v Wade, without any plan for what comes next. Their tactics are not attached to a long-term strategy – and are, in fact, disruptive and destructive for any long-term strategy.

With foaming mouths and red-eyed rage, most pro-life Republican leaders insist on looking just one step ahead.

I don't know why this is hard to grasp: a coherent strategy must look ahead. And looking ahead, a pro-life strategy must be:

- *international, not limited to 5% of those in danger*
- *nonviolent, aiming for peace between generations*
- *organized to grow not shrink, build bridges not walls*
- *respectful of the oldest and wisest leaders and allies – that is, the Catholic Church*
- *responsive to the Gospel*
- *unswervingly committed to an alliance with mothers and prospective mothers*
- *peaceful and protective, not militaristic and domineering.*

Permit me to offer nine brief observations regarding pro-life strategy.

#1: About vision

The pro-life movement in the United States, as it developed after the Supreme Court decisions in 1973, had three main branches: (1) pregnancy aid, or help for women and couples facing an unplanned pregnancy; and (2) education; and (3) political and legislative (and judicial) efforts to restore legal protection for unborn children. Since the 1970s, I have argued that a fourth branch is necessary – not as a minor addition, but as the heart of the whole movement. That fourth branch is nonviolent direct action, which was later called the "rescue" movement. These ideas are set out in *Emmanuel, Solidarity: God's Act, Our Response.*

I have also argued that the *educational* work of the pro-life movement is misguided. A key problem is that we have misunderstood our opposition almost completely, for decades. The opposite of a pro-life position is not a pro-choice position; it is, rather, eugenics. Pro-lifers have argued that life begins at conception, and demanded that "pro-choicers" explain when they think life begins. That question makes sense to pro-lifers, but does not make sense to a huge portion of the world. If you accept that the *question* makes sense, then the pro-life *answer* also makes sense. But if you believe that life is a continuum, then there's no clear "beginning," and the question makes no sense. So we babble past each other.

This total misunderstanding of our opposition, going back decades, suggests that we haven't been listening. We have taken a reasonable position, and repeated it over and over. It *is* a reasonable position – but it's based on unstated assumptions that are not shared by everyone. So our position, however reasonable it is, remains completely irrelevant to many people, who have long since abandoned any effort to engage in serious dialogue with us, because they think that we are incurably narrow-minded and dogmatic. It's impossible to carry on a dialogue with people who refuse to listen. These ideas are set out in *Roots of Racism and Abortion: An Exploration of Eugenics.*

I argue also that the *political* approach of the pro-life movement has been misguided. Just as our educational approach has been narrow and insulated from contact with real challenges, so also our politics has been narrow, based on purity and not outreach. We have worked with like-minded people, and denounced people with other views. This habit has reduced us bit by bit, and now most pro-lifers are content to seek a mere affirmation of slogans, without much subtlety. This has made it possible – in fact, easy – for unscrupulous demagogues to manipulate us.

And indeed demagogues found us out. In the 1960s, Republican strategists discussed how to respond to the ideas embraced and taught by the Second Vatican Council, the whole "Social Gospel." The challenge was that the Democratic Party seemed to be in tune with the Council in many ways, seemed to be the obvious vehicle for those who wanted to press forward toward peace and justice. To avoid watching the whole Catholic Church move as a block into the Democratic Party, Republican leaders including Pat Buchanan – an early and prominent advisor to President Richard Nixon, and a neighbor of mine – urged that the Republicans respond to this existential threat by focusing on abortion. If the Republicans had a monopoly on the pro-life movement, that would answer the Democrats' claim to be the voice for peace and justice. Buchanan et al were prepared to split the Church in order to rescue Nixon's party.

It is my view that the pro-life movement must be rebuilt, from scratch. It must be based squarely on a solid foundation of nonviolent action. It must understand and respond to eugenics, and stop fussing about feminism. It must set out to grow, building alliances and coalitions that are as broad as possible, not as pure – and narrow – as possible.

I understand that these positions of mine make me a pariah in the Republican-dominated pro-life movement. But I have a vision of a pro-life future, and a strategy for getting there. Do you?

#2: Current pro-life "strategy" is nonsense

It baffles me, often, listening to intelligent pro-life leaders explaining what we need to do. Almost all the time, they assume without explaining that reversing *Roe v. Wade* will end abortion. But will it? Asking people to examine this assumption is like attacking Scripture or explaining the flat earth or banning chocolate: many pro-lifers just can't face the question. But it's urgent.

We have to face it. Erasing *Roe v. Wade* is likely to save some lives, but it's possible that it won't save a single life. Reversing *Roe* doesn't provide legal protection of children; it just sends the question back to the states. Some states will enact protective laws immediately. But some won't – not in the foreseeable future, and not without the help of a reformed Democratic Party. If *Roe* disappears, anyone anywhere in the country who wants an abortion can still get one, although it may require more travel time, which may be a nuisance and may mean extra expenses.

The semi-strategy that grips the minds of most pro-life national leaders is a cheap solution. And like all cheap solutions to complex social evils, it will fail.

It is possible that abortion in the middle of the country will be seriously inconvenient, that women or couples between the Mississippi and the Rockies will have to figure out how to get to Denver for an abortion. Women in west Texas or North Dakota seeking abortion will face serious new obstacles – a long day's drive in each direction, perhaps, plus lodging for a couple of nights.

That, friends, is the sum total of the current goal of the pro-life movement, stated honestly. That's not protection; it's just bragging rights (among pro-lifers) in the states that make abortion inconvenient.

You can blame that on the Demon-crats, which is fun. But the fact remains, you have gone as far as you can go without their help: abortion costs more, and it's less convenient. Period.

That's your *victory*? Are you kidding?

Tell me if I'm wrong. Tell me what prominent pro-life leader is speaking honestly about the difference between protecting babies and reversing *Roe v. Wade*, and is explaining how to protect children nationwide, after *Roe* disappears.

The current "strategy," if we can call such a short-sighted effort a strategy, is to get rid of *Roe*. To do that, the pro-life movement is determined – is desperate! – to get pro-lifers on the Supreme Court. I hear that part. I understand it. But then what?

If you demonize and alienate all the Democrats in the country in order to get your pro-life Supreme Court, what's your next step? You haven't ended abortion, and you have absolutely no chance of passing protective laws in last 15 or so states. You have erected new barriers to growing the movement, and now you are stopped dead, far far short of real protection. If you reverse *Roe*, you still have to pass state laws, everywhere – which means, with some support from the people whom you chose to demonize. The demons refuse; that's their nature. So you fail. Oops.

And that's the current dreamy thing that stands in for strategic planning, the silly semi-strategy that's lodged firmly in the back of the minds of most pro-life leaders.

#3: Dump the Dems, dump the nation

The hemi-demi-semi-strategy isn't just silly go-nowhere nonsense; it's also divisive and destructive.

The simplest criticism of a pro-life Democrat is the judgment that it seems impossible – or almost impossible – to persuade the Democratic Party to return to its former pro-life stance. And if the party can't be changed, then a Democrat who remains in the party is choosing freely to stay with a pro-abortion organization. Right?

That sounds sensible.

However, isn't is also clear and obvious that persuading the *nation* to return to its former pro-life stance also seems impossible, or almost impossible? Aren't the challenges involved in persuading Democrats to adopt a pro-life stance similar to the challenges involved in persuading the nation to do so?

Actually, no. They aren't "similar." They're the *same*.

If you say that it's impossible to change the Democratic Party, that includes another tacit assertion. You're also saying that it's impossible to change the *country*, that we will always fail or even step aside when children are in danger. You are announcing your opinion that change isn't possible, that the pro-life movement has failed permanently.

Unlike you, I fully intend to work towards a pro-life nation (and world). I don't expect to see it in my lifetime, but I haven't given up. You have – and you demand that I give up too. You don't really believe that the pro-life movement can succeed – and then you have the gall to denounce me as a traitor because I haven't given up. That strikes me as a little weird.

A single party can tinker with the law and make temporary changes. But to make a deep and permanent changes, we need to get other major parties on board. This is not a complicated idea.

If you want a national change, then changing the Democratic Party is unavoidably a part of the work. If you've given up on the Democrats, you've given up – period.

When someone has a plan and it fails, it can be embarrassing to switch to plan B. But people do it all the time, so pro-lifers can make a switch, right? Yes, perhaps – but not easily. Our Plan A, as executed, included burning bridges. So we're not back to the beginning; we're way behind the old starting line.

For decades, the annual March for Life was led by Nellie Gray, a proud and tough attorney from DC. I enjoyed that lady! She was courageous, inspiring, and decisive. Like any real leader, she made some flawed decisions, but she wasn't arrogant. I admired her. However, part of her standard spiel was disastrous, and we have to go back to it and reject it. She insisted, for years, to wild applause: "I will not negotiate with baby-killers." She worked hard to deepen the division between those who protect the unborn, and those who don't. Her intent was to ostracize – and it worked, but not quite the way she intended. Pro-lifers are not the majority; we are minority, and we are ostracized. So we are still making our demands for changes in society – but now we make the demands from the fringe, or even as outsiders. And that was our choice. We demanded division, and got it. It's worthless; it's destructive; and it's ours.

In your despair, you're not just wasting time on tactics that will fail; you're also making it harder to implement a real strategy. You're not just biting the hand that you will need to feed you; you're gnawing it off and spitting it in our faces. That's a dumb strategy, and you oughta cut it out.

And: NO, I will not join you in your despair.

#4: Movement by movement, state by state

The unexamined assumptions of the pro-life movement today include that the key to the struggle is political, involving national and state politics. I reject that assumption: I think politics – that is, electoral politics and legislative or judicial changes – is secondary (or third or fourth). But when I agree to focus on politics, and try to listen to pro-life leaders and cooperate, I'm not on the same page: why are they fixated on national politics, not global? And even when I agree to set aside global issues temporarily, and to focus (for now) on national politics, I'm *still* not on the same page as most pro-lifers. National politics is shaped by what happens state by state, *but also* by what happens movement by movement.

Often, state-by-state politics *reflects* what people are thinking. By contrast, it's often movement-by-movement politics that *changes* what people are thinking.

If you want to change a nation, you can struggle to elect the right people, state by state. That's not stupid – but it's not the *only* way forward, and it's not necessarily the *best* way forward. For example, if you had to make a choice – that is, you had to decide where to allocate money and time – would you rather win Illinois or the labor movement? Would you rather win California or the feminist movement? Texas or the peace movement? New England or immigrants? Sure, it does make sense to think about how to win state by state; but it *also* makes sense to think about how to move forward movement by movement.

Take Eagle Forum, for example. When I was working full-time to build pro-life nonviolent action, Eagle Forum came after me. Around 1980, the Pennsylvania chapter gave uncomplimentary awards to Juli Loesch and me. I forget the exact details, but one of us got the Benedict Arnold Award, and the other got something like the Judas Award. They didn't like us. Why not? We were solidly and undeniably pro-life! The problem was, Eagle Forum was anti-abortion – but was also involved in fights about feminism and nuclear weapons. I worked loudly and proudly with people on both sides of those national debates – but my own view was clear. I thought (and think) that sexism was an evil that was eroding away in our time (as Pope John XXIII said in *Pacem in Terris*); I considered myself a pro-life feminist. And I thought (and think) that nuclear weapons could not be used with "discrimination" (that is, avoiding civilian deaths) and – following Vatican II – that the indiscriminate destruction of civilian populations was a crime against God and man that "merits unequivocal and unhesitating condemnation."

So my views on peace and justice were a challenge to Eagle Forum: true enough. But not to the pro-life movement!

So why did Eagle Forum work hard to get rid of the peace activists and feminists *in the pro-life movement*. Who was helped by that?

Cooperation was (and still is) possible. I started pro-life sit-ins (later called rescues) in New England. Our first action was at Planned Parenthood in Norwich. Around the same time, I was also arrested at Electric Boat in Groton, CT, protesting the construction of nuclear subs. Much of the preparation for the sit-in at Planned Parenthood – weekly meetings to pray and reflect on Isaiah's "Songs of the Suffering Servant" – were in the kitchen of an engineer who worked at Electric Boat. So I was arrested at his work site, but he and I were still able to cooperate in planning a sit-in at Planned Parenthood.

The pro-life movement can and must – and once did – bridge gaps. We need veterans and peace activists. We need feminists and traditionalists. We need environmentalists and industrialists. Writing off one movement after another was a disastrous mistake after mistake.

To expand, the pro-life movement must break free of the stranglehold of any narrow partisan who wants to coopt us – in this case, the Republican right.

#5: "Decruiting" obvious allies

One of the dumbest blunders in American history is still unfolding slowly right now. The pro-life movement, in desperate need of allies, is deliberately alienating 30-40 million potential allies. What great strategic plan includes such lunacy?

To me, it seems obvious that a determined movement with a serious mission will work to expand, not shrink. To protect children (in the USA for a start, but then the world), we need to build a solid social consensus that life begins at the beginning, not in the middle. But most pro-life leaders today are intent on a specific political strategy – to protect the unborn, we have to change the law, and the only way to do that is to change the courts, and the fastest way to do that is through a determined and muscular Republican majority. And the Republican majority is anti-immigration (or pro-slow-immigration). So pro-lifers must join the GOP (and cooperate with its savage inhospitality), and then make sure the party is uncompromising.

That's not 100% pure crazy, but it's close – maybe 99.44% crazy. It's ignorant and un-democratic. It's ignorant: this strategy – change a massive entrenched social evil by education leading to legislation – has no precedent in history, which suggests strongly that it's impossible. But also, it's un-democratic, and I want to focus on that for a moment.

I'm puzzled about how it happened, but it seems to me that pro-lifers have lost track of an idea that's basic to American history.

Decisions in a dictatorship don't require persuasion and cooperation and coalition-building, but decisions in a democracy do. Our nation is based on ideas about equality and human rights – and liberty. As a nation, we don't believe that the legitimate power to govern is delegated by God to a king. We are committed to the idea that the authority of a government, to be legitimate, must be based on the will of the governed. The people rule – through leaders they choose, for sure – but the ultimate authority on earth belongs to the people. To make a deep and permanent change in the law, ending a massive and deeply entrenched evil, we need a campaign of nonviolence that changes hearts and minds of the rulers – the people. That's first, logically and chronologically. In a democracy, we persuade and cajole and build coalitions based on respect and cooperation. That's how democracy works.

And that means, if we are going to work within a democracy and not in a dreamland, then we need to expand. And indeed, it seems to me, we have an obvious opportunity to expand that we must seize, not discard. The culture of Latin America is changing, but it is not yet as thoroughly pro-abortion as our culture. And Muslim socety is under systematic pressure from eugenicists promoting abortion, but Muslims – in general, globally – are not as likely to promote abortion as post-Christian Westerners. So it would make sense to me to work carefully and deliberately to recruit Latino and Muslim and other immigrants. We have about 30-40 million potential allies in each generation of immigrants. Do we want their help?

It is stupendously stupid to ally ourselves with xenophobes! We are not just neglecting a massive opportunity to recruit; we are, as a movement, working hard to de-cruite! We are allied with people who want immigrants to stop coming here! In fact, we are combing the country for millions of people – our natural allies! – to send away!

Like King Canute, xenophobes work to reverse an unstoppable tide. That's stupid and destructive. But also, from a sharply focused pro-life perspective – momentarily neglecting the God-given right to migrate and focusing only on how to expand the pro-life movement – we are engaged in an effort to *deport our allies!*

Pro-lifers might as well erect billboards at the border: "Pro-lifers, we hate your guts! Go away!" That is our message to the children of Guadalupe – who are pro-life until we decruit them.

Why do pro-lifers do this?

#6: Single issue silliness

For decades, most pro-lifers have fended off the approach taken by the Catholic Church to abortion. That is, most pro-life leaders have avoided requests for consistency – and have denounced the "seamless garment" approach. Pro-lifers have said that we are and we must be "single issue." I think this has been a grave strategic mistake. But more simply, I think it's nonsense: the pro-life movement has *never* been a single-issue movement. From the beginning, the pro-life movement has *always* addressed multiple issues.

Consider.

The pro-life movement in the 1970s had a manual that covered a lot of ground fast – what conception and embryonic and fetal growth look like, what the different methods of abortion look like, and a list of associated questions. This pocket-size manual, Jack Willke's *Abortion Handbook*, was the principal teaching tool of the movement for a decade or two – and it covered abortion *and euthanasia*. It was principally about abortion, but the decision to include euthanasia helped to make clear that we were "pro-life" and not just "anti-abortion." The movement insisted that we fought to protect humans "from conception until a natural death." Abortion and euthanasia: that's two different issues. That's not *multi*-issue, because two isn't quite multi; but it's not *single*-issue either. The major national organization, National Right to Life Committee (NRLC), used Willke's handbook, and his approach. So did the first large splinter group, American Life Lobby (later American Life League).

There was an influential organization in Minnesota that took a somewhat different approach. The Human Life Center (HLC) emphasized that Planned Parenthood had moved from advocating contraception and criticizing abortion to advocating both without much fuss and bother. They emphasized that abortion is rooted in an attitude toward human sexuality. They argued that if you accept that sexual activity is private matter, and that its meaning is up for grabs, you get around to abortion very quickly. If sex and birth drift apart in theory and in practice, with sex for fun and IVF for babies – and if we accept an apparent commonsense proposal that good fun can't cause great damage – then abortion follows. So they opposed the contraceptive mentality as well as abortion. HLC's approach was common – not as common as the NRLC approach, but not rare – and it was even less single-issue.

I mentioned Eagle Forum above. They were a well funded and well organized piece of a conservative coalition – and a major player in the anti-abortion movement. They were multi-issue: anti-abortion, anti-feminist, and pro-nuke. That particular conservative coalition is still visible and vibrant, although it's changed a smidgeon: now it's anti-abortion plus anti-gay and pro-gun.

Pro-life liberal coalitions didn't thrive. Rev. Jesse Jackson, before he turned pro-choice, said that the mentality of slavery and the mentality of abortion are the same: treating a person as a thing. It was an interesting argument, but it remained just a debater's argument, and never became much of a coalition. (Ask Jesse why not.)

Similarly, many pro-lifers compared abortion to the Holocaust, for two reasons. First, abortion produces corpses that end up in the waste stream, or in labs, or in crematoria. Second, and much more important: abortion involves killing huge numbers of people while society looks on and refrains from interfering. However, many Jewish leaders, including pro-life activists, expressed strong and principled opposition to this linkage, and it never became any kind of coalition.

In the early 1980s, Juli Loesch championed a "consistent" life approach, embodied in the organization she founded, Prolifers for Survival. They (we) opposed abortion and capital punishment and nukes. This idea was embraced by Cardinal Joseph Bernardin, who spoke about a "seamless garment." Now the idea is carried forward by the Consistent Life Network.

Conservatives promote a single-issue approach when they want leftwingers to go away. But the movement has never been single-issue. Never.

#7: Make gestures, or changes?

When I worked with Human Life International, one of the hard lessons I learned was about how many "pro-life" leaders were intent on changing laws, just laws, without any regard for actual practice, without regard for real babies and real mothers. In Mexico, for example, abortion was illegal, but was also advertised openly in the *Paginas Amarillas*, the Yellow Pages. So what did pro-life leaders want? Enforcement? Nonviolent direct action? No, no, no. Pro-life leaders, in general, were content to protect their toothless, meaningless, hypocritical *laws*.

Faced with a slaughter, do pro-lifers want to make gestures, or make changes? That is, do we want to wave a flag and talk to each other? Or do we want to engage with our fellow citizens and work to change minds and hearts?

One of the clearest examples of this choice was when the Me Too campaign got underway. It was not a pro-life initiative, but it did get at the some of the roots of the abortion movement, and pro-lifers should have supported it. The abuse of women is among the most powerful forces pushing towards abortion. Me Too challenged that force. Where were we?

Pro-life leaders often support chastity education, pushing back against the idea that sex is natural and delightful and everybody should play. Pro-lifers have struggled to re-assert an ancient idea that sex is related, somehow or other, to babies, and therefore probably belongs within the context of conscious and future-oriented commitment. Great idea! But can we do it? Can we make that idea common and influential again? Probably not, or not any time soon – but Me Too got halfway there.

When John Paul II was pope, I read his weekly meditations that became the basis of his "theology of the body," and I thought it was all brilliant. And I accept the teaching of Gandhi, that peacemaking requires self-control – in his words, that "brahmacharya" (chastity) is indispensable in a campaign of "satyagraha" (nonviolence). Gandhi was not a flower child. Great ideas, but how do we get from here to there? In post-Christian America and Europe, nonproductive sexual activity is deeply rooted and flourishing, like kudzu. And in many countries – including Saudi Arabia and India, recently prominent examples – there's a rape culture producing unplanned babies. The obstacles are daunting.

The Me Too campaign stood up against that rape culture. It challenged male domination and sexual oppression, and made a real impact. India is visibly changed, and even the Saudis have taken notice of the global changes that are underway. Sure, I'd like to do more: Me Too is about consent, not chastity; it has nothing to say about consensual extramarital sex. But from a pro-life and pro-family perspective, it is such a huge step forward! Where were we?

Pro-lifers who have spent time outside abortion clinics have seen coercive abortion unfolding. A car pulls up, an angry guy gets out and grabs a crying woman, and pulls her along. You hear the shouts: "We arready talked about this and we're gonna get it done now, goddammit." This doesn't happen every Saturday morning at every clinic, but it's common. Sometimes a pro-life agenda and pro-choice agenda flow together: if the woman can choose, the child can live.

The whole Me Too campaign was about freedom from such oppression.

Where were we?

#8: Corrupting even pregnancy aid

Is it true that the Republican Party is pro-life and the Democratic Party is pro-abortion? I say no, that's nonsense. Look at pregnancy aid.

The healthiest part of the pro-life movement is pregnancy aid – thousands of volunteers offering their time, their cash, their homes, their everything-they-got, to help women and couples facing an unplanned and for now unwelcome pregnancy. I admire these folks, immensely. However, even this healthiest part of the movement is undercut by the pro-life movement's links to Trump and his savage opposition to immigration.

Around the world in 2020, there are 65 to 70 million people on the road, fleeing from war or gang violence or rape or starvation. These refugees and stateless persons and homeless migrants are not welcome in the USA. Before Trump, about two million people came into the country annually, half with legal documents and half without. Trump has worked hard to bring that number way down – fighting "illegal" immigration, and reducing legal migration by half, and even working to trim our welcome for refugees – refugees, for God's sake! – to a few thousand annually. Amidst the worst refugee crisis since World War II, the wealthiest continent refused to participate in building and maintaining safe havens.

There's a detail in the refugee crisis that is significant to the pro-life movement: that 65 million refugees includes about a million pregnant women. A million pregnant *refugees*: need they say more to be considered women facing crisis pregnancies? But these million women in crisis pregnancies are not welcome within several thousand miles of a proud American crisis pregnancy center. And what do American pro-lifers have to say about this scandal? Nothing. Our crisis pregnancy centers are for Americans, not for foreigners. With eyes wide open, American pro-lifers support Trump's decision to turn away a million pregnant women carrying a million babies, in crisis.

How can you help them? Not all refugees want to go to America, believe it or not. But some do, from Latin America, and they show up at our southern border. They don't need diapers; they need advocates who will help them get across the border and out to family or friends or employers. To put this another way: if you support Trump's decisions about Latinos coming north – a blanket ban instead of effective and efficient screening that keeps out criminals but lets in pregnant moms – you oppose pregnancy aid.

Millions of refugees are stuck in camps in Jordan, Lebanon, Turkey, and elsewhere. You can support the United Nations High Commissioner for Refugees. They aren't anti-abortion, but they will help women in crisis. To put that another way: if you are so paranoid about Socialism that you think the UN is demonic and you won't cooperate with the UNHCR, you oppose pregnancy aid.

Do you want to help pregnant moms in Africa? Support Catholic Relief Services. To put that another way: if you are paranoid about CRS, you oppose pregnancy aid.

Do you want to help moms in concentration camps in China and North Korea? Nancy Pelosi, not Trump, has had her eye on forced abortion for 30 years. It's hard to pressure those brutal governments, but it's not impossible; it has been done. By Pelosi. In other words, if you refuse to cooperate with Pelosi, you oppose pregnancy aid.

I understand that what I'm saying isn't popular among pro-lifers. But when you look at the plight of pregnant refugees honestly, it seems that the pro-life movement has abandoned its mission, even the clearest and purest part of its mission – pregnancy aid.

It used to be simple for pro-lifers: if there's a pregnant mom and an unborn child in danger, drop everything and help, because nothing matters more. But now, there's a higher priority. Mother and child in danger? Um, are they refugees? Then walk away.

#9: Consistent ethic of hospitality

I've been working since 2012 to link abortion and immigration. I was startled when I saw the huge gap between what Scripture and the Catholic tradition say about hospitality, on one hand, and what people think about it on the other. It seems to me that most people consider hospitality to be a decoration, like flowers on the table, not a matter of immense and eternal significance, like justice and truth. I think we need to explore the idea of hospitality, including the many links between abortion and immigration.

First, the next generation comes from two sources. The next generation in the USA (or anywhere) will come from (1) births and (2) immigration. To shape the future of a society, you want to control these two sources of new life. And so the eugenics movement, a conscious effort to construct a new and improved human race, set out to control both as effectively as they could. And in fact, restricting immigration in the 1920s and expanding abortion in the 1960s were major accomplishments of the eugenics movement. The link: these are the sources of the next generation.

Second, the proponents of two campaigns of savage inhospitality are the same people. The eugenics movement in the 1920s launched three major initiatives:

- sterilizing the "feeble-minded,"
- outlawing "miscegenation" (marriage between people of different ethnic backgrounds), and
- restricting immigration.

The sterilization campaign damaged tens of thousands of people, then receded. The anti-miscegenation campaign was part of the nation's savage racism, but it too was beaten back. The anti-immigration laws stayed in place. And then in the 1960s, members of eugenics societies in Britain and the USA launched – and led, funded, housed, and promoted – the abortion movement.

Both immigration restrictions and abortion are about hospitality to people who show up in our lives on their schedules, not ours, capable of altering our lives substantially even if inadvertently. On one hand are the unknown un-named unborn, and on the other are the undocumented unwashed displaced.

Third, it is almost impossible to construct an argument for restricting immigration that isn't also an argument for global population control. (That is, in brief: the argument for restricting immigration is that we can't help all these poor people; it's too much of a burden. But you might notice: we are richer than most of the world, so if we can't afford to help, the rest of the world really really can't.) And global depopulation schemes include forced abortion. In other words, restricting immigration in the USA – the global haven for refugees for the past several centuries – leads to more abortion overseas. Reports of increased miscarriages among pregnant women being held for deportation are horrifying in themselves; but they are only the tip of the iceberg.

Fourth, both abortion and restricting immigration are ways to turn away from the creative initiatives of the Lord, who always cherishes us but also, almost always, challenges us. When the uncomfortable Other shows up in our lives, we are invited to meet God. In the carefully repeated words of Jesus, "Whatsoever you do for the least of my people, you do for me." In Scripture, when angels show up, they always say, "Do not be afraid," because people are *always* scared. These words apply when any celestial messenger – or baby, or stranger – shows up. We are always startled, puzzled, worried, afraid – always. And the Lord asks us to trust him – always.

Fifth, Scripture links abortion and migration. Many pro-lifers find a call to care for the unborn and for worried or disturbed or reluctant mothers in the words about care for widows and orphans throughout Scripture and history. But in the Old Testament, we don't find just a pair, widows and orphans. Almost every reference to this pair includes a third; it's a trio, not a pair. Of the 21 references to widows and orphans in the Bible, 18 refer to widows and orphans *and strangers*. The Lord demands that we intervene to help (1) mothers without supportive husbands, and (2) children without caring parents – and also (3) anyone without a home, without a supportive society.

Immigrants and babies change our lives – but the changes, on balance, are joyful and delightful and enriching and wonderful, now and forever.

Part II: Culture of Life

Most of my thinking about how to protect unborn children and help pregnant mothers is shaped by the teaching of the Catholic Church. That approach exposes me to the argument that I'm trying to enforce my own narrow religious views. I deny that: if I can't make arguments in favor of protecting children that non-Catholics understand, then my work will fail – and should fail. In a pluralistic society, you have to be able to explain your goals in ways that people of other faiths or no faith can understand. But I repeat, for those who want to trace my thinking about how to proceed, it usually begins with and is largely shaped by my faith in Jesus and my determination to understand and follow the teaching of the Catholic Church.

The Catholic Church is not, and should not be, tied to a political party. But in my thinking, I find that the approach of the Church to moral issues draws me to the Democratic Party at its best. The Church's approach is global, not nationalistic; it is consistent, not single-issue; it is generous and loving, not legalistic and restrictive.

I admit freely – and in fact enthusiastically – that other people shaped by the Church will be drawn to Republican Party. All the great political and social arguments of our time are reflected in religious arguments within all healthy religious communities. But to understand my political views in any depth (should you wish to do so), you need to understand how my faith shapes my views.

It's often pretty simple. In brief: I embrace the immense challenges that are found in the teaching of the Second Vatican Council. I embrace the teaching in the Compendium of the Social Doctrine of the Church, the Catholic version of the Social Gospel, which includes the teaching in the Gospel of Life from St. John Paul II.

Protecting the lives of the helpless is a universal responsibility, shared by all people of good will.

Permit me to offer a short essay and ten observations about Catholicism and abortion.

#10: John Paul II's freeing concept

In conversations about race, there's often a huge disconnect, like the great line from *Cool Hand Luke*: "Now, what we have here is a failure to comyoun'cate." Pope John Paul II describes a conceptual tool that may help to bridge this significant communication gap.

Perplexed individuals who have been accused of racism may review their personal histories, and insist truthfully that they have never used the N-word. That's good! But can we get serious now? Racism is structural, and that structure does damage even without crude insults. JPII explains this. His concept is not exactly the same as the language of "structures," but it's close.

He said that there are some grave evils that cannot be brought to light by a mechanical search for some technical violation of the Ten Commandments. He spoke of "social sin." To think clearly about abortion or racism or many other evils, you need this idea, in some form.

In his revolutionary teaching about making peace and changing destructive habits (specifically in his apostolic exhortation "Reconciliatio et Paenitentia," #16), he offers four definitions of "social sin," and then uses one of them. The four:

1.   Every time you do wrong, it affects everyone, directly or indirectly, because our spiritual lives are all interconnected in different ways, some obvious and some mysterious. So all sin is "social." True, but very broad and kinda vague.

2.   The Lord spoke of two commandments: love God and love your neighbor. Every violation of the second commandment can be called "social." Also true but also broad and kinda vague.

3.   Sometimes there are breaks between various human communities. These are evil. To call them "sins" requires some explanation: calling war a "sin" may be more of an analogy than a definition. But this is the meaning that the Pope chooses to employ.

4.   Sometimes people try to analyze things that go wrong, attributing the evil to uncontrollable structures; no individual is responsible. Terrible things happen, but no one did it. The Pope dismisses this fourth use of the phrase as a worthless fraud.

Back to the third meaning. There are breaks in society that are evil, that we need to talk about as evil. He lists examples (in a previous section, #2):

- violating human rights
- violating conscience
- racial or religious discrimination
- terrorism
- torture
- nuclear weapons and the arms race
- unjust distribution of wealth and power

Who does these things? Who "distributes wealth unjustly"? Sure, it happens, but when and how and who's responsible?

JPII says that "such cases of social sin are the result of the accumulation and concentration of many personal sins."

So what do people actually do that adds up to these social sins? He says,

"It is a case of the very personal sins …
- of those who cause or support evil or who exploit it;
- of those who are in a position to avoid, eliminate or at least limit certain social evils but who fail to do so out of
  - laziness,
  - fear
  - or the conspiracy of silence,
  - through complicity
  - or indifference;
- of those who take refuge in the supposed impossibility of changing the world and also
- of those who sidestep the effort and sacrifice required, producing specious reasons of higher order.

The real responsibility, then, lies with individuals."

So what does racism look like, if it's not an actual lynching, not shouting the N-word? Well, JPII says it might be more simply "taking refuge in the supposed impossibility of changing the world."

You can't get at this profound evil in a legalistic fashion. You can't haul someone into court for the crime of "taking refuge in a supposed impossibility." And you can't get at this thing in a Baltimore-Catechism-trained confession: "Bless me, Father, for I have sinned ... I took refuge in a supposed impossibility."

Social sin is hard to get at legally, or legalistically. But the concept points the way toward reform and/or repentance. Did we hide behind a claim of helplessness, a supposed impossibility? We did. I did. Can we stop it? We can. I can.

This approach has huge strengths and advantages. The language of social sin points to the future, not the past. It speaks of us, not of me. It points to healing and hope, not to shame. It makes it possible to take responsibility without trying to accuse oneself of criminal behavior.

The way out of social sin is not by prosecuting and jailing the perpetrators. It's not by "three Hail Marys and a good Act of Contrition." It begins with understanding the deeply rooted problem and recognizing the humanity of its victims, and then acting in solidarity with them.

Racism exists, and it kills. But who did it? Did "I" do it? I'm inclined to deny it. Does that mean no one did it, that it just happened? That's crazy. Or was it just a few bad actors, like the KKK? That's just not real, and we all know it; there's more to the story. But if it's not me and it's not them, who did it?

Did "we" do it? Of course "we" did! So let's stop it!

"Social sin": clear thought helps build peace.

Social sin, defined

St. John Paul II, *Reconciliation and Penance*, 16

Whenever the church speaks of situations of sin or when she condemns as social sins certain situations or the collective behavior of certain social groups, big or small, or even of whole nations and blocs of nations, she knows and she proclaims that such cases of social sin are the result of the accumulation and concentration of many personal sins. It is a case of the very personal sins of those who cause or support evil or who exploit it; of those who are in a position to avoid, eliminate or at least limit certain social evils but who fail to do so out of laziness, fear or the conspiracy of silence, through secret complicity or indifference; of those who take refuge in the supposed impossibility of changing the world and also of those who sidestep the effort and sacrifice required, producing specious reasons of higher order. The real responsibility, then, lies with individuals.

#11: Catholic Church: pro-life, pro-justice

I'm a pro-life Democrat, and a Catholic who embraces the whole teaching of the Church, whether it seems to be from the left or the right. And I note an interesting detail about the Church's teaching about abortion: the key documents from this teaching are all written within a context and in a language that are congenial to "seamless garment" liberals.

The Second Vatican Council, in *Gaudium et Spes* (*The Church in the Modern World*), published in 1965, refers to abortion twice. Paragraph 27, within the section on "The Community of Mankind," is a "seamless garment" presentation. It has abortion in a list of evils that includes "murder, genocide, abortion, euthanasia or willful self-destruction." The list includes assaults on life itself, but also assaults on human dignity, such as deportation. On the other hand, paragraph 51, within the section on marriage and family, speaks again of abortion and infanticide, this time in the context of sex and love and chastity. That's two contexts: one is of the liberal peace-and-justice variety, and the other of the conservative personal-morality variety. In the Church's teaching, *both* are there.

Humanae Vitae, the 1968 encyclical from Pope Paul VI that turned his reputation upside down, transforming an ultra-lefty into the rock of the right, is about birth control, not abortion. But many pro-lifers use it extensively. So it's worth noting that he raises three key concerns. Most of the encyclical is an argument about morality, but he also makes three social predictions in paragraph 17, warning about consequences. One is a familiar slippery slope argument, generally congenial for rightwingers: he says that a mentality that accepts contraception will soon accept other forms of immorality. Second, he says that a contraceptive mentality will make it easier to treat women as objects, mere instruments for the satisfaction of a man's desires. This argument is generally dismissed by feminists as factually wrong, but the *concern* is based on lefty feminism. Third, he points to the risk of totalitarian abuse: what is permitted may become mandatory. The concern here is about social justice. That is, Pope Paul's arguments include a moral code argument that pleases conservatives – but also a feminist plea, and then a social justice perspective. Even in "Humanae Vitae," he is not a knee-jerk predictable rightwinger.

Pope St. John Paul II did the same kind of thing when wrote about family life in his apostolic exhortation on family life, *Familiaris Consortio*. He denounces abortion, and discusses it within the context of a "contraceptive mentality." But also, in this document that pro-lifers flourish, he speaks about the rights of migrants and exiles and refugees. He declares (in paragraph 46) that families have a *right* to migrate in search of a better life. So it's loopy to try to box him up as a liberal or as a conservative; he's both, or neither, or transcendent, but not one or the other.

The key pro-life Catholic document of our time is, of course, St. John Paul II's 1995 *Gospel of Life*. Here too, the teaching of the Catholic Church is placed carefully in a broad context, in a seamless garment context. In paragraph 3, he repeats the teaching from *Gaudium et Spes*, considering abortion within a list of grave evils, assaults on human life and dignity, including – I repeat – "poverty, hunger, endemic diseases, violence and war," and "murder, genocide, abortion, euthanasia, or willful self-destruction" and "arbitrary imprisonment, deportation, slavery, prostitution," among others.

The teaching in key Catholic pro-life documents is firmly embedded in the language and approach of social justice.

#12: Virgin of Guadalupe: a voice of unity

In 2009, Hillary Clinton, then serving as the Secretary of State, visited Mexico. While she was there, she made her way to the shrine of the Virgin of Guadalupe. The rector of the basilica brought the image down from its usual place above the altar, so that she could examine it closely. She looked it over a bit, and then asked, "Who painted it?" She was mocked by her detractors for that question. I never understood that mockery. I would gladly sacrifice an arm for the opportunity to explore that life-transforming question with her.

The story of how the image appeared is powerful, if you can believe it. And if you can't believe the story (look it up), the image is still beautiful and detailed, although it's on a rough fiber – on a peasant's cloak. The technique to produce it is still not understood. The colors are not paint: there's nothing between the fibers. And they are not dye: the back of the cloth is blank. And if you can't accept the story, and don't care about the technique, you're still left with its impact: the image is extraordinarily eloquent in its pictorial messaging. In 1531, after a decade with the conquistadores, nearly all the people of Mexico remained baffled and unimpressed by the Spaniards' explanations of God. But the clear ideas conveyed by the image resulted in the prompt and permanent conversion of millions of people.

Don't miss this! Ireland was brought to Christianity by St. Patrick. Germany was converted by St. Boniface. The Slavs listened to Sts. Cyril and Methodius. But Mexico! Mexico's claim about their primary evangelist is astounding! They received the Gospel from Mary.

The message of Lourdes is about healing, and something about the Immaculate Conception. Fatima is about repentance and prayer for Russia. The messages are a bit complex, requiring explanation. But the Guadalupe message is ultra-simple: I'm with you.

So she's with someone – but who? Was she speaking to Mexicans, or Central Americans, or all the people of the Americas? Everyone? Initially, she spoke to the indigenous people of Mexico: she looked like them, not like a Dutch Renaissance blonde; she spoke to them in their language, and the rest of us need a translation; and the messages built into her clothing and posture and gestures were all sharp and vivid in that culture, not ours.

The Virgin of Guadalupe was not a part of the life of Catholics in the United States in my generation. I attended excellent Catholic schools for 12 years, and – to the best of my recollection – the first time I heard this story was when I was 22. The National Shrine of the Immaculate Conception in Washington has an impressive collection of images of Mary from all over the world, in the side altars throughout the basilica. The Mexican image is in one of the smallest alcoves. The people who built the shrine knew about Guadalupe, but it wasn't a priority for them.

But Latinos knew her. When Cesar Chavez was organizing farmworkers, he led marches and demonstrations that used two principal symbols. One was the logo of the United Farm Workers, the angular black eagle that was stamped on lettuce picked by the UFW. The other was the image of the Virgin of Guadalupe. The workers – including Mexican immigrants, many undocumented – thought that she was with *them*.

And American Catholic pro-lifers today think she's one of *us*.

Indians and conquistadores, peasants and scholars, farmworkers and pro-lifers: the Virgin of Guadalupe bridges gaps, and unites us.

#13: The unity of the Catholic Church

On the night of the Last Supper, the night before Jesus was crucified, he prayed for the unity of the Church. To me, that seems to imply three things: (1) the unity of the church is immensely important; and (2) it is likely to be extraordinarily difficult, perennially bordering on miraculous; and (3) it will come about. So I am committed to the unity of the Church, as the express desire of the Lord and as something valuable in itself, but also as a prerequisite to many other works undertaken by the Church.

In my lifetime, the Church's work for unity has been extraordinary. The Second Vatican Council included a determination to end several bitter divisions: the split between Christians and Jews, the split between Western Catholics and Eastern Orthodox, the split between Catholics and Protestants, and the war between Christians and Muslims. We have a mixed progress record on ending these ancient divisions, but the work that's underway is astounding.

Sadly, though, even as we set out to heal ancient rifts, we tore open a new division – between the left wing of the Church which emphasizes the social Gospel, and the right wing of the Church which emphasizes personal morality. Having a left and right is healthy and normal, when the two sides cooperate. Splitting them is destructive: each of us has two arms and two legs and two ears and two eyes, but only one head and one heart.

A prominent detail of the current division is the split between pro-lifers and pro-immigration activists. To me, it seems blindingly obvious that they go together in a consistent ethic of hospitality.

The unity of the Church is expressed and confirmed in the Eucharist, the Mass. Catholics assert their belief that the bread and wine we share at Mass is in fact the body and blood of our Lord. This isn't the time or place to explain transubstantiation, but I want to look at two implications of it.

The Catholic Church asserts that a zygote, a newly fertilized ovum the size of pencil dot, is a child of God and a member of the human family. That's not obvious to the naked eye. But if you feed and protect a zygote, there's just a short time – maybe nine months, if you're fussy about what you see – before this entity becomes easily recognizable. Is it hard to believe that a tiny thing, smaller than a mosquito's head, is a brother or sister? Of course it is. But if you are accustomed to the belief that a small piece of bread becomes the body of Christ, then laying hold of the idea that embryos are family is easy.

On the other hand, we are also accustomed to looking for the Lord in his needy people. St. John Chrysostom was eloquent about seeing the Lord in the poor: he said that if you don't see the Lord in the beggar at the door of the church, you won't find him in the chalice.

It seems to me that these two assertions belong together. The Lord comes to us in tiny children and in needy strangers. The Lord invites us to see *both* truths, and to cooperate with each other.

This has a political implication. We almost certainly cannot protect babies without Democrats, nor welcome immigrants without Republicans. We need pro-immigration Republicans and pro-life Democrats.

We need unity.

#14: Global fight against population control

The eugenics movement organized in America in the 1920s to improve the human race by social control of reproduction, breeding "more children from the fit, less from the unfit." This included sterilizing the "feeble-minded." But by far, the most important part of this vast human engineering project was the drive to reduce the number of "colored" people, mostly overseas, by population control. And the most dramatic example of population control was NSSM 200, a 1975 document which defined black babies in Africa as threats to our national security, alongside Russian bombs and Chinese Communists and Cuban propaganda. (See #21 below.) When you see how much work the USA has done to drive down the world's population, you realize that abortion within the USA – a million babies annually – is a small fraction of the real problem, the global bloodbath – which is more like 40 or 50 million dead babies annually. American pro-lifers usually fixate on 2-3% of the dead.

The global fight doesn't resemble the national fight. Let's look at three examples – the campaign to resist sterilization in Puerto Rico and then two United Nations conferences on population.

First example: In the 1930s, American industrialists wanted a cheap and stable work force. Puerto Rico was cheap, but wasn't stable; the people were poor and restless. So American employers set out to stabilize the work force by reducing family size there, by sterilization. Catholics were already fighting eugenic sterilization in all 48 states, and they went to work in Puerto Rico. But they were beaten back soundly – until pro-choice feminists also organized to protect women. Catholics and pro-choice feminists cooperated in Puerto Rico, and won.

Second example: I covered the International Conference on Population in Mexico City in 1984 for the *National Catholic Register*. At the opening press conference, I asked the executive director of the United Nations Fund for Population Activities (UNFPA), Rafael Salas, why his organization was giving awards to the Chinese and Indian population programs, which were openly coercive, neither pro-life nor pro-choice, neither pro-child nor pro-woman. He huffed and fluffed, and later hunted me up to chat a bit – but didn't answer.

A pro-life coalition was present and active at the Mexico City conference, resisting UNFPA's agenda: the Americans (led by Alan Keyes), and the Vatican – and Latino nations and Muslim nations. A spokesman for the Vatican told me that the coalition was familiar; that same group had been in the same fight ten years before at another UN population conference, in Belgrade. Latinos? Muslims? In general, what is the attitude of pro-life leaders towards Latinos and Muslims today?

Third example: Ten years later, there was another UN conference on population, in Cairo. A similar coalition formed to resist, but this conference recalled events in Puerto Rico. Pro-lifers in Cairo worked to distribute information about NSSM 200, the shocking American population control document. In this effort, pro-lifers cooperated again with pro-choice feminists who despised coercive policies.

My point is simple. American pro-lifers today are generally ignorant about the global fight. In their ignorance, they have aligned themselves with eugenic anti-immigration activists (in John Tanton's tribe), and attacked their true allies, including the Vatican, Latinos, Muslims – as well as, on some occasions, pro-choice feminists.

For decades, the global pro-life coalition has included the USA, the Vatican, Muslims, and Latinos – with pro-choice feminists collaborating against coercive depopulation. But Republican pro-lifers want nothing to do with that.

In fact, they don't even want pro-life Democrats!

#15: Culture of life, civilization of love

There's a phrase that became a slogan for the pro-life movement – "to build a culture of life, a civilization of love" – that comes from St. John Paul II's encyclical, *The Gospel of Life*. Are we still planning to build one? I'm still committed, but truly I have no idea how many other pro-lifers have the foggiest notion what the Pope said.

In paragraph 91, he writes about population control, and he denounces coercive abortion (all abortion, but coercive abortion in particular), or any coercive measure to limit birth. No surprise there. But then he offers a non-coercive response to the "population problem." He writes: "Governments and the various international agencies must above all strive to create economic, social, public health and cultural conditions which will enable married couples to make their choices about procreation in full freedom and with genuine responsibility." Wait a minute. Who did he say is supposed to create these economic and social conditions? "Governments and various international agencies."

It gets more intense: "They [these governments and international agencies] must then make efforts to ensure 'greater opportunities and a fairer distribution of wealth so that everyone can share equitably in the goods of creation. Solutions must be sought on the global level by establishing a true economy of communion and sharing of goods, in both the national and international order.'" Say again? He said that a pro-life response to population problems includes *governmental* efforts towards a *fairer distribution of wealth*. That's from St. John Paul II, the notorious Commie (?).

Mike Schwartz, a great pro-life leader and speaker and activist for decades, used to talk about "poverty" and "overpopulation," noting that the two words refer to the same thing – an imbalance goods among people. But the first word sounds like something that Jesus asked the rich to fix, and the second word sounds like something stupid that poor people did. They broke it; they fix it. Schwartz was echoing the teaching from the Lord, from Scripture, from St. John Paul II, challenging us to see that talking about overpopulation can lead us away from our roots.

JPII's encyclical continues, asserting that pro-life work "also appears as a providential area for dialogue and joint efforts with the followers of other religions and with all people of good will." Ecumenism! And even cooperation with atheists! Oh my God!

Two weeks after the bloody events of 9/11, at a meeting with Muslims in Kazakhstan, Pope John Paul II spoke about cooperation in building a civilization of love. "From this place, I invite both Christians and Muslims to raise an intense prayer to the One Almighty God whose children we all are, that the supreme good of peace may reign in the world. May people everywhere, strengthened by divine wisdom, work for a civilization of love, in which there is no room for hatred, discrimination or violence."

Pope Benedict XVI continued his predecessor's drive for a civilization of love. Speaking to Muslims in Cameroon (March 19, 2009), he said: "I therefore encourage you, my dear Muslim friends, to imbue society with the values that emerge from this perspective and elevate human culture, as we work together to build a civilization of love."

I'm serious about the teaching of the Pope about the culture of life and civilization of love – unabridged. The unabridged version is about social justice, distributing wealth, ecumenism, all this leftwing thought. Further, it includes Muslims prominently.

I accept the Pope's leadership, and this challenge, without reservation. But I wonder, often, if all the pro-lifers who call for this culture and civilization ever read *The Gospel of Life*.

#16: Paraclete: advocate, lawyer, lobbyist

In a healthy nation, we would have parties offering different approaches with different emphases, pushing and shoving a bit but aiming for unity. In a healthy nation, there is tension between money checked by political power, and political power checked by successful business. In a healthy nation, the advocates of individual rights and responsibilities would wrestle with the advocates of social rights and responsibilities. Some truths are obvious from one perspective but obscured from another. We need each other. It's proper that we jostle; we don't have to despise each other.

With that in mind, I'd like to offer two rather different interpretations of a Gospel story. I embrace both. I note that one is easier for Republicans to grasp, and the other is easier for Democrats to grasp.

Personal model

The story of the Good Samaritan offers a model of hospitality. A man is mugged, and lies by the side of the road, bleeding. A civic leader comes along and sees him. His view is that he must take good care of his immediate family, then his circle of good friends, then his neighbors; but the roadside victim isn't on any of his standard lists. So he passes by. Then a religious figure who runs several welfare agencies also sees the bleeding man. But he can't figure out which bureaucracy should handle this problem, so he too goes by. A third man, an outsider, sees and hears the man in trouble, and stops to help. He stops the bleeding, binds the wounds, and moves the man to shelter. He pays for food and nursing care for a few days.

Jesus deals with us with tenderness, in a one-on-one relationship, ensuring that the basic needs of life are met. Be like that, he says.

Social Gospel model

Another reasonable interpretation builds on Moses and puts the needy individual in the center.

Moses insisted that we should welcome strangers, because –

remember! – you too were once a stranger in a strange land. Memory should stir compassion. Similarly, in Jesus' story, the Good Samaritan, who knows what it's like to be ignored, sees the man's plight and promptly imagines himself in that situation. Imagination should stir compassion. The Samaritan, like the solid citizen, has a set of circles of responsibility in the back of his head; but the center of the circles is the man in trouble. Is the victim's family here? Nope. Are his friends here? Nope. How about his neighbors? Hm. What's a neighbor? When that desperate man looks at me, does he see a neighbor? He hopes so, but does he? It's up to me to decide.

The victim is central: what does he need? Food? Then get it. Nursing? Then get it.

Suppose he need a legal advocate? If that's what he needs, then I should help him get a lawyer. Suppose he needs a new immigration policy? If that's what he needs, get it!

That approach can lead right to the whole social Gospel.

So the parable has at least two plausible applications. You don't have to choose; you can embrace both.

#17: The treasures of the Church

I don't think that St. Lawrence was a Democrat – truly I don't. But as a Democrat, I find his understanding of "treasure" to be congenial.

The story is, during some great persecution, the emperor swept up all the prominent leaders of the church in Rome, and sent them off to kingdom come. A deacon named Lawrence took responsibility for leading the living remnant. Then the bloody-minded oppressors demanded that Lawrence collect the treasures of the church and surrender them all. Lawrence agreed to do so, and showed up in due time at city hall – with all the blind and lame and broken of the city: in God's eyes, and Lawrence's, the treasures. The powerful lords of the city were unamused; they roasted him. He died, the story goes, cracking jokes: "Turn me over! I'm done on this side."

I think of Lawrence and his treasures when I hear Republican leaders talking about immigration policy. It's not just their savage inhospitality that baffles me; it's also their brutish stupidity when they are faced with God's Treasures.

I do not understand people who assume that every sensible American agrees that we want to keep out immigrants who arrive with needs. Many Republicans are willing to debate about how many educated immigrants with credentials and skills should be allowed in. But generally, they assume that we need to screen out the freeloaders who are hoping to get someone in the family into an American hospital. By contrast, the Church asserts that migration is a right – a right, belonging to individuals and also to families. If a worker wants to immigrate, and has family members with special needs, why should that be an obstacle? Immigration policy isn't just some kind of employers' recruitment plan; it's the immigrant's right. And the sick are a treasure!

Recall the struggle when President Obama was working to get his Affordable Care Act through Congress. He hit a startling roadblock. In the final weeks of negotiations, the Catholic Church – which had been pressing for universal health care for a century – opposed the final draft of the bill. They had concerns about abortion and protection for conscientious objectors. But also, they opposed it *because it excluded undocumented immigrants.* That's my Church!

Is an immigrant who needs medical care an expense or an epiphany? In the totally insane American health care "system," patients can run up six-figure hospital bills very quickly. But Jesus – the Lord of the universe – said: when I was sick, you helped Me. Is that true? Is it relevant?

I'm not opposed to encouraging people to get medical help in their own countries – as long as we (Americans) are serious about foreign aid packages – through the government or through other organizations – that ensure that poor nations can provide competent health care. But we *aren't* serious; we dabble and dribble, fuss and delay. Turning away sick immigrants reveals an attitude toward immigrants – and also toward the sick.

Look. If you don't see Jesus in the sick, you don't see him at all. And if you think you do, you are dangerously deluded.

I stand with St. Lawrence and Pope Francis. Receiving health care is a right; providing health care is a privilege.

#18: Six red flags at the border

In his teaching about the last judgment, Jesus gave us six invitations, six injunctions. Feed the hungry, give drink to the thirsty, welcome the stranger, clothe the naked, visit the sick, visit the imprisoned – and enter the kingdom of God. What? Why? Because you cared for Me, says the Lord. Alternatively, don't feed the hungry, don't give drink to the thirsty, don't welcome the stranger, don't clothe the naked, don't visit the sick, don't visit the imprisoned – and go to hell. What? Why? Because you didn't care for Me, says the Lord.

That's pretty clear. So what are we doing at the border?

People show up at the border, fleeing from violence or poverty. Many of them are hungry, or were recently and will be again soon. And thirsty. And they are, obviously, strangers. That's three red flags flying. Are the red flags for Christmas: Look, Jesus is here? Or are they red for warning: danger?

They are red for a choice. Choose life.

Some of the hungry thirsty immigrants aren't dressed properly for the weather: that's a fourth red flag. Some are sick: that's five.

Our response, often, is perplexing, and dangerous as all Hell opened wide: we lock 'em up. That's the sixth bright red flag. How can we be so stupid? I don't understand how Christians overlook what's unfolding, what's waving in our eyes.

Many pro-lifers have a checklist of grave evils in hand. It's not the same as the list from Jesus. What they are concerned about is a list of five "non-negotiable" items: abortion, euthanasia, embryonic stem cell research, human cloning, and homosexual marriage. And none of those are going on at the border, it seems, and so pro-life leaders opt to be neutral. That's really strange, to use a checklist that was developed a few years ago *instead of* the Lord's own words!

But actually, it's worse than weird! Most national pro-life leaders are *not* neutral about immigration; they actively *support* the savage inhospitality of the Trump administration.

And worse still: abortion *is* an issue at the border. There are pregnant women among the refugees and migrants. Globally, there are about a million pregnant women, homeless and wandering or even fleeing on the roads of the world. And some are at our border. Is there a pro-life response to these crisis pregnancies? Nope. Most pro-lifers are quite willing to go along with Republican leadership, and work hard to keep these women out, lest they give birth to anchor babies. If they are born here, those babies become citizens here, and they might bring their families here one day. So pregnant women get special attention from Republican pro-lifers: it is especially urgent to *keep them out.*

So at the border, six red flags fly – but Republican leaders ignore them. And abortion is an issue – but pro-life leaders go along with a determined effort to keep crisis pregnancies out of here.

The angels who ate with Abraham at Mamre are the same ones who destroyed Sodom. Those angels rewarded hospitality, and they punished complacent inhospitality.

O Angels of Sodom, draw near!

#19: Pro-life passages: all pro-immigrant

I have been fighting against abortion since 1972, when I was doing alternative service as a conscientious objector during the war in Vietnam. During these five decades, I have spent a lot of time thinking about the passages in Scripture that refer to unborn children – in Isaiah 49, Psalm 139, in all mentions of God's special protection of orphans, in Luke's Visitation story, and in Matthew's Holy Innocents story. I find these passages inspiring, pregnant. However, when I started looking at Scriptural teaching about welcoming strangers, I didn't find a scattered handful; I found hundreds of passages. When a pro-lifer uses Scripture to talk about abortion but not about immigration, that's a problem. It's unbalanced and biblically illiterate.

And I note: *All the pro-life passages are also pro-immigrant.*

Consider Isaiah 49: "Before I was born, the Lord called me, from my mother's womb he spoke my name." When Isaiah says this, he is speaking to *foreigners*: "Hear this, *distant nations*." And Isaiah's mission, from his mother's womb, is not just to the people of Israel; he is a light to the *Gentiles*, to all people to the ends of the earth. He is a voice calling the Israelites back from *exile*.

Consider Psalm 139: "You knit me together in my mother's womb." The Lord's words are addressed to a wanderer, a *fugitive*: "Where can I run from your love?" Nowhere in the universe is hidden from God.

Consider all the passages about God's special protection of widows and orphans – which pro-lifers apply to mothers without family support and babies without parental protection – that is, to mothers and babies at an abortion clinic. Of the 21 passages in Scripture referring to widows and orphans, 18 are about a trio, not a pair: widows and orphans *and strangers*. The Lord cares for people without national protection.

Consider the Visitation, when the fetal John dances with joy at the coming of the embryonic Jesus. The setting for the story is *hospitality*: Elizabeth and Mary, host and guest, coming together in mutual love and admiration.

Consider the story of Herod's massacre. It begins with some mysterious *foreigners* from the east making a pilgrimage to honor the newborn king. How they knew, and how much they knew: this remains mysterious. But these *strangers* were invited by God. Further: the allusion to Rachel, the lamentation in Ramah, is her wailing for her children who had been killed *or driven into exile*. Further: The story ends with the Holy Family going into *exile* in Egypt. Pope Pius XII said the exiled Holy Family is "for all times and all places, the models and protectors of every migrant, alien and refugee of whatever kind." Matthew's remarkably poignant story of a threat to helpless babies is also a remarkably poignant story of *exile*.

The plight of threatened unborn and despairing mothers cannot be separated from the desperation of refugees and exiles. These are different details of a single reality. Our response must be a consistent ethic of hospitality with a welcome for all strangers, including the unborn.

#20: The "non-negotiables"

One of the most bizarre developments in the pro-life movement in the past few years has been the emergence of a list of "non-negotiable" items. The idea is weird: is this a political term, or a business term, or what? It's not standard in any discussion of justice or morality that I know of. Even in politics or business, what's wrong with negotiation? Further, the items that made the list are weird, and some are definitely negotiable. But the biggest problem, it seems to me, is what this list seems to replace. The idea of the list, I think, is that some issues of right are wrong are clear, and we can't bend on them. Okay, I get it, I guess. But this list doesn't resemble the Ten Commandments: are they negotiable? It doesn't resemble the Sermon on the Mount. Negotiable? It doesn't resemble the Lord's fiery injunctions in his sermon on the Last Judgment. Negotiable? It doesn't resemble the teaching from Vatican II or in St. John Paul II's encyclical, *The Gospel of Life*. Negotiable? So what is this new list?

It has five items: abortion, euthanasia, embryonic stem cell research, human cloning, and homosexual marriage. It does not have contraception.

Euthanasia has gray areas. When you decide whether to continue a treatment – for example, penicillin for pneumonia when the patient has terminal cancer – the moral question turns on your *intention*. Are you permitting the natural process of death, or are you deliberately hastening death? That's complex – negotiable.

No serious Catholic moral theologian objects to embryonic stem cell research, unless it's (1) human, and (2) destructive. Putting this item on the list was sloppy.

Some fertility treatments are likely to result in twins. That's a form of cloning. And in fact, it's the only form of human cloning currently going on. Like most Americans, I would oppose cloning by somatic cell nuclear transfer, and it is a real threat on the horizon. But why put it on this list if no one is doing it?

And if you do want to put cloning on the list, a part of the moral issue here is separating sex and procreation: contraception is sex without procreation and cloning is procreation without sex. I wasn't there, but I think the non-negotiators negotiated on contraception and backed off prudently.

Human cloning can involve life and death. President Clinton's bioethics board argued that human cloning wasn't horrible unless you produced cloned adults, and they advised proceeding with human cloning but killing the embryo at about two weeks. But the non-negotiable list – at least in the Priests for Life version – doesn't include any arguments against this "clone-and-kill" policy.

So what's this gibberish list all about? What's it for? I think the attraction of it is that it's divisive. "Unconditional surrender" and "no compromise" and in fact "non-negotiable": what fun to say! It doesn't get anything done, but it separates one side from another, and lets the dividers feel tough.

When pro-lifers opt to divide, they just ostracize themselves. Which is non-useful.

I prefer Matthew 25.

Part III: Republican Failures

I try hard to be a good bridge, but sometimes this bridge is in flames.

From 2016 to 2020, the pro-life strategy – protecting children by changing the law, without much in the way of other changes – has been tied tight to Donald Trump. I don't think this smells good. I don't this is realistic. I don't think this is sane.

I think that true change focuses on politics near the end, after many other changes.

I think that restoring a social commitment to protecting the lives of the helpless requires leaders who value the lives of all the helpless – leaders who are men and women of courage and generosity and integrity and justice.

I think that unifying a nation in a renewed commitment to protect the helpless requires a serious effort to bring together all people of good will.

I think that renewing a generous love of the unborn requires intelligence and imagination and kindness.

I agree that the Democratic Party needs reform, that most of the party's leaders at this time are deeply committed to abortion as a fundamental right, and that's a serious evil. I do not dispute that. But I think that the Republican Party is in far worse shape.

I look forward to a time when Democrats and Republicans will listen respectfully to each other and make decisions based on shared values.

But for now, let me be clear about the troubles that I see in the pro-life movement and especially in its Republican leadership. Permit me to offer ten overlapping vignettes and observations.

#21: The attack on African babies

"National security": that's seven syllables for war, State Department jargon for the things that America will fight for.

National Security Study Memorandum 200 – NSSM 200, mentioned above – was a classified document initiated during the Nixon administration and adopted by the Ford administration. It was instructions to American ambassadors around the world, making sure everyone was on the same page. It explained the dangers that we saw on the horizon, the threats to our safety as a nation.

First, there were Commie nukes.

NSSM 200 was written before the fall of the Soviet empire. Russia and America had huge weapons systems pointed at each other, and that was the greatest threat to American national security. The military had principal responsibility for pushing back against that threat.

Second, there were Commie dominoes.

The United States fought in Vietnam from 1955 to 1975. NSSM 200 was written shortly before we flew the last helicopters out of Saigon. During and after the war in Vietnam, there was some concern about a "domino" theory. Eisenhower, in the 1950s, had expressed the worry: China turned Communist, and then there was a war in Korea. Would Vietnam be next "domino" to fall, to be followed by Laos and Cambodia, then Thailand, Malaysia, Indonesia, Burma (Myanmar), and India? Some people worried that the falling dominoes might topple all the way to Australia. So NSSM 200 asserted that we saw a threat to global peace – and to our national security – around the "Pacific rim." And again, the military had principal responsibility for pushing back against this threat.

Third, there were Commie shoots.

The threat in Latin America was "incipient" Communism. Castro ruled a Communist Cuba, and he was working throughout the continent to stir up revolution. The United States supported a collection of military dictators who were committed to suppressing

Communism there. The Central Intelligence Agency (CIA) had principal responsibility for pushing back against this threat.

Fourth, there were ... well, it's a little hard to explain.

The threat in Africa, as perceived by the Nixon and Ford administrations, wasn't Communism – with nukes, or toppling, or incipient. No, the perceived threat there was population growth. Growing populations could make poverty worse, which could lead to instability, which could lead to chaos, which could lead to revolution. Africans killing Africans is an African problem, not a direct threat to American security. But the continent has abundant natural resources as well as abundant people. We wanted access to those resources, and so revolutions there were a threat to us. So NSSM 200 asserted that our national security depended in part on avoiding chaos by avoiding instability by avoiding poverty – by controlling population growth. The Agency for International Development (AID) had principal responsibility for protecting us from that threat, from the teeming masses of black babies.

The threats to us, as seen by the American government under these two (Republican) administrations, were:

- Commies with bombs in Europe,
- Commies taking over Asia,
- Commies trying to take power in Latin America, and
- black babies.

Population control: that means contraception, sterilization, and abortion. But how do you sell that in cultures where family life is central – where people love the life of busy little scurrying children – where babies are understood as joys, not burdens?

When you set out to transform cultures at their roots, the lines between advertising and propaganda and warfare get blurred.

AID prepared and funded a long list of propaganda programs. They paid a popular musician a full and generous year's salary to write one song about small families. They hired non-Muslim scholars to explain how the Quran supports contraception. They recruited and trained community leaders and doctors, and educated them in America. Everywhere, they included depopulation programs in aid packages – modern medicine with sterilization.

This is racism. This is neocolonialism. This is psychological warfare. And when Africans learned about NSSM 200, they were not well pleased.

Roe v. Wade was and is a very serious problem – for the nation but especially for the Democrats. But NSSM 200 was and is much bigger, far worse, killing far more – and it was and is a Republican problem.

#22: The great divide

When the pro-life movement first became a serious national force in response to *Roe v. Wade*, there was no glaringly obvious partisan split. Democrats were as likely as Republicans to be pro-life. Pro-lifers who wanted to build grassroots outreach campaigns were likely to start with their friends who were already organized – in labor unions. But there was already a serious change underway, and understanding that change matters.

Start with the Second Vatican Council, a Catholic event, that ran from 1962 to 1965. It was extraordinarily ambitious, a conscious effort to transform the Church's manner of engaging with the rest of the world – including a determined adoption of the Social Gospel and an equally determined rejection of antisemitism and other forms of religious bigotry. The Council didn't change any fundamental teaching about who the Lord is or about what the Gospels say, of course; but it did change the way Catholics thought about how to *implement* the Lord's teaching. A key document, entitled *The Church in the Modern World*, asserted that the Church would be engaged in work for peace, for justice, for human rights, for civil rights, for workers' rights, for women's rights (which did not include abortion). This was a change, responding to the signs of the times.

The Council ended in 1965. (Implementing the Council, of course, continues to this day.) But then in 1968, there was another complex event that appeared at first to be interesting but not especially influential – but which turned out to be a significant counterbalance to the whole Council. Pope Paul VI, who presided over most of the Council and devoted his life to making it work, published an encyclical about birth control, "Humanae Vitae." In doing so, the Pope pulled off an amazing acrobatic stunt: without budging an inch, he moved from the far left to the far far right (in the view of many people).

The changes proposed in Vatican II posed a serious threat to conservatives within the Republican Party, which was at that time less assertive than Democrats about civil rights. The party couldn't write off the whole Catholic Church and survive; they had to compete for Catholic votes. They had to adjust (that is, repent) and embrace social justice including civil rights – or they had to find some way to blunt the impact of Vatican II. They did not opt for repentance. Instead, they found that a way to counter the Council – by clawing their way toward a pro-life monopoly. "Humanae Vitae" was a rallying point.

To survive after Vatican II, Republicans had to divide the Catholic vote. So what they did was straightforward: they worked hard to set peace and justice activists against pro-lifers. They made pro-life and pro-family noises, and in 1968 they captured a majority of the Catholic vote, and Nixon won the election.

To consolidate that victory, Republicans have had to work hard for decades on three tasks. (1) They needed a response to the pro-choice voices within the Republican Party: drive them out or limit their impact. (2) They had to respond to the millions of pro-life voices in the Democratic Party: coax them out or limit their impact. And (3), they had to respond to the inconvenient teaching of Vatican II, which was consistent, pro-life and pro-justice: that had to divide the Church to match American partisan politics.

This wasn't good for the country, nor for the Church, nor for the truth, nor for the unborn. But it was good for Nixon and the Republican Party. So Republicans divided the Church.

Balance matters. It is certainly true that there were social justice advocates who supported abortion rights, the flip side of the pro-lifers who opposed the struggle for social justice. I lived for a while in Weston, Massachusetts, and my Congressman was a Jesuit priest, Fr. Robert Drinan. He was a prominent proponent of a broken version of a "comprehensive" approach to social justice – ignoring abortion.

In my view, embracing abortion rips the guts out of a drive for social justice.

- I estimate that abortion is about 90% of the lethal violence in the nation. Abortion was often defended by social justice advocates who proposed that we "make love, not war" – and then clean up the complications of "love" violently.

- I note that abortion is personal, one-on-one – not impersonal like war.
- I believe that abortion alters family life. A mother makes a violent decision about her own child. And dad is excluded from the decision.
- It's my view that abortion guts feminism as a force for peace and justice, as a force for nonviolence.
- It seems to me that embracing abortion lards the whole project of social justice with hypocrisy.

Nonetheless, when I look at the catastrophic chasm between pro-lifers and social justice advocates, it seems to me that what Pat Buchanan (and others) did was far worse than what Fr. Drinan (and others) did. In my view, abortion was and is the largest and the bloodiest evil of our time, the most personal and yet simultaneously the most globally devastating of the social justice issues. Drinan's dissent was about an unimaginable slaughter. And yet, it is also true, in my view, that the pro-abortion arguments were *dissent*, while the assault on social justice teaching was *schismatic*.

Drinan (and others) rejected an *encyclical*. But Buchanan (and others) rejected a *Council*.

Drinan challenged the Church's teaching *on an issue*. But Buchanan trashed the Church's *authority to teach*.

Drinan wanted to *change Church teaching* on a core matter. But Buchanan wanted a *different church*.

I believe that abortion was and is the worst horror in our history, but I am convinced that *finding our way out of the slaughter depends in large part on a unified church*. I do agree that Democrats bear more responsibility for abortion today than Republicans, but I think Republicans have closed the way out of the evil.

In any case, I won't cooperate with this crazy division. I am Catholic – that is, both pro-life and pro-justice. I want a pro-life Democratic Party, and a pro-justice Republican Party. I want a unified Church, and a unified nation.

#23: Contrast in a parish

Pat Buchanan, a conservative Republican leader and one-time candidate for President, denies that he promotes racism. Let me paint a picture. I want to contrast what my father did and what Pat Buchanan did.

Pat Buchanan grew up in Blessed Sacrament parish, on the border between Maryland and DC, and so did I. He's a decade older than me, but one of his brothers was a classmate of mine. In his autobiography, he talks about scenes and characters who were a part of my life too. I knew the guy with brain damage that Pat makes fun of. I knew the fence around a country club where he and friends tossed a drunk buddy for temporary storage. And I knew what it was like in the parish when the nation and church were desegregating.

Blessed Sacrament School was not quite lily white: there were some Italians there. There was a family there with Spanish in the background, but they were from Spain, not Latin America. White.

When Archbishop O'Boyle showed up in DC in 1948, he went to work right away to end segregation. He was cautious and systematic, but determined; he avoided confrontation, but integrated all the parishes and schools before the 1954 Supreme Court desegregation mandate in *Brown v Board of Education*. Still, northwest DC was white.

My father supported Archbishop O'Boyle. He worked at Army Map Service, where – attentive to the call for justice – he hired the first blacks, and not to do maintenance. He needed mathematicians, so he administered a test on math (mostly on quadratic equations). There were a lot of black men around who were qualified but had faced discrimination for years; when they competed on level field, they did best, and my father hired them.

My father supported the archbishop again, when O'Boyle supported Martin Luther King and persuaded President Kennedy to let civil rights activists use the Lincoln Memorial for his March on Washington. My father joined the march, proudly.

A quick vignette from the 1960s. In about 1965, there was a knock at our front door. It was a black man collecting signatures on a petition for fair housing – in Chevy Chase. My father invited him in, and they chatted a bit, and then my father asked who in the neighborhood had signed so far. No one. He asked if he could go with for the rest of the evening. The visitor agreed, so my father put on his coat and they went out together. And then everyone – at every single door where they knocked – signed.

This was a time of transition, when the difference between complete failure and complete success in an endeavor could turn on a small act. Is a neighborhood 100% for fair housing, or 100% against? In the middle of a change, a little push at the right moment can make a big difference.

In the 1960s, during this time of transition in the Church and in the country, what was Pat Buchanan doing? He was on the other side, cracking racist jokes. When the Church worked to change its approach to race from top to bottom, Pat dissented. He threw snowballs at black women. Just some whores, he explains in his autobiography.

In the middle of a change, a little push at the right moment can make a big difference, for better or worse. A few signatures here, a few snowballs there. Little things.

In these little things, Buchanan rejected the teaching from his pastor Msgr. Roach, from the Holy Cross nuns who taught in his elementary school, from his Jesuit high school teachers, from his Jesuit college professors, from Washington's Archbishop O'Boyle, from all the Popes of his lifetime, and from the Pope and bishops teaching united in a Council.

Was he a racist? Because he threw snowballs?

No. He was a racist because he grew up in a lily-white community, which is okay; but then – when the Church repented and changed, and the nation reconsidered and changed – Buchanan refused to change.

Racism isn't just lynching. Usually, it's about what we fail to do. It's hard to understand that unless you have in your head some intellectual tool like "structural racism" or "social sin." It's hard, but the tools are available.

#24: Hypocrisy: NSSM 200 and *Roe v Wade*

During the Nixon administration, there were two abortion-related actions of immense significance: the decisions of the Supreme Court in *Roe v. Wade* and *Doe v. Bolton*, and the preparation of National Security Study Memorandum 200. The Court's decisions were not Nixon's decisions, not Republican decisions nor Democratic decisions. And the responses were not partisan; both Democrats and Republicans across the country responded with a mixture of horror and applause. But as years and decades passed, the Republicans captured the leadership of the pro-life movement in response to *Roe*, and Democrats slipped slowly into an increasingly solid pro-*Roe* stance.

But NSSM 200 was far more deadly than *Roe*. It put the United States firmly into the business of global population control. Our policy was not explicitly pro-abortion; it promoted depopulation without specifying measures. But the world was moving toward depopulation by contraception plus sterilization plus abortion. China and India were leaders in coercive abortion, but many other nations adopted some level of coercion. The global abortion rate, according the research branch of Planned Parenthood, the Alan Guttmacher Institute, reached over 50 million annually, approaching 60 million. So what was happening within the USA – where the abortion rate after *Roe v Wade* climbed steadily toward 1.5 million – was just two or three percent of the global total.

NSSM 200 was not bipartisan; it was a Republican initiative. It was not the work of the Supreme Court; it was the work of the executive branch. The study was initiated under Nixon, and adopted as policy under his successor, President Gerald Ford.

What I want to emphasize is that while Republican leaders were increasingly critical of abortion inside our nation, they were simultaneously supportive of deliberate depopulation efforts, including abortion, overseas.

It is true that in the 1980s Republicans took steps to oppose abortion overseas. In 1984, under President Reagan, the United States adopted the "Mexico City Policy": the USA would not fund organizations that performed or actively promoted abortion as a method of family planning. But when this policy was announced at the United Nations meeting on population in Mexico City (hence the name), Reagan's Ambassador to the Economic and Social Council (ECOSOC) of the UN, Alan Keyes, led the fight there, working with a group that may seem startling today: Latin American nations, Muslims, and the Vatican. So the fight was *not* *isolationist.*

Further, the fight in Mexico City included two pro-life approaches – not contradictory, but quite different. At that meeting, the UN Fund for Population Activities (UNFPA) announced awards to China and India for their "effective" work to reduce population growth. When Rafael Salas, executive director of UNFPA, welcomed journalists from around the world and outlined what to expect, the first question he got focused on coercion: was UNFPA holding up coercive programs – which were anti-life and anti-choice – as models for the rest of the world? This was pushback against UNFPA, and was an invitation to anti-coercion feminists.

The Mexico City Policy was good, and it was a Republican initiative. But it's about funding. It's a significant interim step, like the Hyde Amendment, which might affect 5% of abortion. But opposing coercion is another interim step that's far more important. Resisting coercion could affect 30% of abortion, globally.

NSSM 200 was hypocritical and deadly, and the Mexico City Policy did not reverse it.

#25: Catholics in GOP reject Social Gospel

Pope Leo XIII wrote an encyclical about labor in 1891, *Rerum Novarum*, that had an immense impact on the Catholic Church, initiating a century of thought and teaching that transformed the Church. Pope Leo's successors wrote encyclicals based in part on his thought, some of them named explicitly as anniversary letters – the 40th, 80th, 90th, and 100th anniversaries of *Rerum Novarum*. That teaching was fundamental to the work of the Second Vatican Council. And it was collected in 2004 in the *Compendium of the Social Doctrine of the Church*, requested by St. John Paul II.

The *Compendium* lists the "the milestones of the path travelled by the Church's social doctrine from the time of Pope Leo XIII," teaching "in the light and under the impulse of the Gospel." That's a proud claim. These milestones include:

Quadragesimo Anno, about justice and ownership;

Non Abbiamo Bisogno, against pagan worship of the State, Fascism;

Mit Brennender Sorge, against neo-pagan myths of race and blood;

Divini Redemptoris, against Communism;

the Christmas Radio Messages of Pope Pius XII;

Mater et Magistra, on human dignity and global unity;

Pacem in Terris, on global peace and justice;

Gaudium et Spes, on the Church's role in the modern world;

Dignitatis Humanae, against antisemitism, for religious liberty;

Populorum Progressio, for a global economy that helps all;

Octogesima Adveniens, on effective action for global justice;

Laborem Exercens, on the dignity of workers;

Sollicitudo Rei Socialis, on the duty of solidarity;

Centesimus Annus, on justice and human rights;

and others.

The Catholic Church claims the authority to teach in the name of the Lord. That's a shocking claim, but we make it firmly. We don't claim that we get everything right all the time, but we do believe that the Lord built a community, and leads it, and that his Holy Spirit shapes the Church's teaching.

Unfortunately, the whole Social Gospel, that whole body of the Church's thought and teaching, from top to bottom, is foreign to many Republicans—either completely unknown, or known and rejected.

William Buckley's *National Review* responded in August 1961 to the Church's teaching about social justice – and in particular in Pope John XXIII's encyclical *Mater et Magistra*, which describes the Church as Mother and Teacher – with explicit and pointed rejection: "Mater si, Magistra no" – that is, "mother yes, teacher no." But I accept the Church's claims about her authority to teach about justice, and I'm not tempted to join the schismatics who rejected the Church's teaching and then deformed the Republican Party.

I have great difficulty understanding why anyone would ask me to join a political party that is full of people who claim to be faithful Catholics but who reject 140 years of teaching, including a Council. I think the rejection of social justice we see today began promptly after the Council, when Pat Buchanan and others sketched a way to protect the Republican Party – by a schism in the Catholic Church.

My position: Mater si, Magistra si. I follow Pope Francis, following the Lord within the community that the Lord started. I accept the Church's teaching on morality and justice, both.

#26: What's the GOP fuss about "socialism"?

Listening to Republicans when they fuss about Socialism is a challenge. I hear them say that they are worried about something that they think is close to godless Communism and outright Satanism. Okay. But this thing they fear is detailed: it includes food stamps for the hungry poor, affordable medical care for all, organized assistance for people overseas, welcome for immigrants – lots of good things. And somehow, this thing they fear *doesn't* include cooperation with Russia, China, and North Korea. Trump, not the Democrats, praises brutal Communist dictators: Putin, Xi, and Kim Jong Un. I can't make sense of their fuss.

The Catholic history of the Social Gospel includes a fiery determination to develop a sense of social justice that makes Communism unnecessary. From Pope Leo XIII to St. John Paul II and Pope Francis, document after document lays out an approach to justice that is solid and vibrant and durable – and anti-Communist. So when you get a generation of Catholics that is split in half – anti-Communist pro-lifers on one side fighting social justice activists on the other side – a part of what has happened here is a schism, even if the schism doesn't show up in Church structures.

It seems to me that Pat Buchanan and Stephen Bannon and Cardinal Raymond Burke are committed to schizophrenia, fiery advocates of rigid ignorance. They don't seem to know the difference between Communism and anti-Communism. They blur and stir, mushing together Communism and Socialism and atheism and the Social Gospel, and Marx and Pope Leo and the Soviets and St. John Paul – the poisons and the antidotes – all rolly-boiled together into a single grey lump of amorphous plastic. How do you get that foolish?

Once you have raised a whole generation of partisans, accustomed to setting pro-life concerns against social justice activism, how do you recover? The answer isn't simple. It's in the *Compendium of the Social Doctrine of the Church*, but what's that? And if you do find it and try to understand it, the first thing you might notice is that it's hefty – a whole lotta words, big fat multi-syllabic kaleidoscopic multi-cultured history-laden words with pages and pages of footnotes.

It's actually not that bad. It has depths, but it's accessible. And it's online, free. And it's arranged in a user-friendly fashion. But you have to want it.

I embrace the Social Gospel, with deep and abiding joy. When I read the Church's social teaching, I come away tingling, more determined than ever to strengthen my little bit of the whole project. I see and love the rock-solid unity of the Church's teaching. And for many people, the Church's teaching is loaded with surprises.

- Were you aware that St. John XXIII supported a welfare state and denounced abortion in the same document?
- Were you aware that St. Paul VI fought the contraceptive mentality and supported the UN?
- Were you aware that St. John Paul II's influential pro-life document, *Familiaris Consortio*, declares that migration is family right?
- Were you aware that his *Gospel of Life* places abortion firmly in a seamless garment context?
- Were you aware that Pope Benedict XVI's concern for truth includes a deep and abiding respect for Muslims?
- Were you aware of how tightly Pope Francis links environmental concerns and pro-life concerns?
- Were you aware that all the Church's extraordinary pro-life teaching is in the social justice *Compendium*?

The Republican opposition to Socialism is a puzzle. They embrace Communists but reject the Catholic Church's Social Gospel! How could I be tempted by such confusion?

I'm a Democrat, and I think I'll stay put.

#27: Pro-life leadership embraces eugenics

A large portion of the pro-life movement used to be against eugenics, "more from the fit, less from the unfit." But I think that resistance is almost all gone.

The problem is not complicated. The *solution* might be extraordinarily complicated, but the *problem* is simple: American health care is expensive, and pro-life leaders have joined Republicans in opposing it.

I am blessed to have a collection of delightful grandchildren. One of them has some challenging medical issues. The problems were detected before she was born, and my daughter's OB-GYN assumed she would promptly schedule an abortion, for obvious eugenic purposes. My daughter was indeed prompt: she dumped that blind brute, and got a pro-life OB-GYN.

That's familiar pro-life territory.

Since her birth, my granddaughter has been expensive: hospitalizations, surgeries, meds, nursing care, specialized equipment. Without the best medical care available in the world, she would be dead. And without Obamacare, her parents could not have provided that care, although they would have gone bankrupt trying.

Most pro-life leaders oppose Obamacare, because – they assert – it's socialist and pro-abortion. But when my daughter chose to keep her daughter alive, all the medical professionals involved got on board right away, with generosity and determination. My granddaughter was born with the encouragement of pro-lifers, but she has been kept alive by all those so-called socialists.

And that's familiar pro-choice territory.

When Obamacare passed, the bishops opposed its final shape. From their perspective, it had three problems: it permitted abortion, didn't have provisions to protect conscientious objectors, and didn't cover undocumented immigrants. Pro-life leaders at the time often distorted what the bishops were saying, and claimed that the bishops opposed the whole idea. That was an error, or a lie; the bishops had supported universal health care for a century, and didn't waver. Demurrals notwithstanding, the bill passed, and Obamacare now provides health care insurance to millions of people – including my granddaughter.

With the bishops, I want some changes in the law – including the three above. These proposed changes would *expand* Obamacare. But Trump – and Republicans cooperating with him, and pro-lifers going along with their allies – are working to *abolish* it. They used to assert that they were going to provide an alternative, a new and improved health care policy. But Obamacare was a compromise from the beginning, and it took years to pull it together. The Republicans couldn't craft a new and improved compromise, and eventually they stopped talking about it. They just want to wipe out Obama's work.

Which would kill my granddaughter.

That's not familiar pro-life territory. But it is the position of most pro-life leaders today.

Ending health care because it's futile is one thing: end-of-life decisions are complicated and messy. But ending care because some people are expensive and not worth it is something else. It's eugenics.

So the pro-life movement today is tied tight to the Republican Party, which is tied tight to Trump, who wants to end Obamacare, which would end expensive health care for millions of people, which is lethal eugenics.

I am a pro-lifer, and I oppose eugenic killing – still. So I'm a Democrat.

#28: Covid-19: Republicans and euthanasia

Take a look at two numbers emerging from the Covid-19 pandemic. It impacts the elderly far more than the young, and it kills blacks twice as often as it kills whites.

As the pandemic took hold, national and international organizations struggled to understand this novel virus. One early insight was about age. Once infected, the death rate for the population as a whole was 1-2%. For people age 65-84, the death rate was 4-11%. For people 85 and older, the death rate was 10-27%. (*Source: National Center for Immunization and Respiratory Diseases (NCIRD), Division of Viral Diseases, May 14, 2020.*)

In May 2020, *MedRxiv*, a preprint service for health sciences, published a report (tentative, unreviewed) that estimated the differences in mortality rates among whites, blacks, and Latinos in the United States. The finding: the death rate among Covid-19 patients for blacks was triple (3.57) the rate for whites, the death rate for Latinos was almost double (1.88) the rate for whites. (*Source: https://www.medrxiv.org/content/10.1101/2020.05.07.20094250v1*)

These differences are interesting, but they require more study and explanation. The higher rate for the elderly may be explained in part by the fact that pre-existing health problems make any disease more dangerous. The higher rates for blacks and Latinos may be explained in part by relatively crowded housing conditions, and by various pre-existing health problems that are more common among blacks than among whites. But whatever the explanation, the data is deeply troubling.

Look at one more set of numbers. Democrats expect the pandemic to be worse than the Republicans expect, and have embraced measures to fight the pandemic far more than Republicans. Is there a 50-50 chance of a second wave, pollsters asked. 99% of Democrats said yes; 41% of Republicans said yes.

The poll asked whether respondents were taking various steps to respond to the pandemic:

- Are you taking precautions like handwashing? Democrats: 96%. Republicans: 83%.

- Engaging in "social distancing"? Democrats: 96%. Republicans: 62%.
- Avoiding crowds? Democrats: 94%. Republicans: 49%.
- Wearing a mask in public? Democrats: 93%. Republicans: 44%.
- Sheltering at home? Democrats: 83%. Republicans: 32%.
- Delaying large purchases? Democrats: 41%. Republicans: 18%

(Source: CNBC/Change Research poll, May 20, 2020)

What does a pandemic have to do with political party? Why is the difference so large and obvious? It seems to me that party leadership and partisan news sources shape people's views. President Trump and Fox News have minimized the problem.

Regarding the race issues, Democrats see a startling measurement of life or death disparities – that are apparently affected by housing, nutrition, medical care. The pandemic seems likely to strengthen previously held views about providing social services.

But the data about age diverges from previously held views. If the pandemic kills the elderly, one might expect pro-lifers – who have been hollering about abortion *and euthanasia* for half a century – to dig in and demand prompt action, effective intervention, and new protections. But they aren't budging.

That's new, and tragic. Republicans – including most pro-life leaders – are less protective of the vulnerable elderly than Democrats.

I'm a pro-lifer, opposed to euthanasia. So I'm staying in the Democratic Party.

#29: Families at the border

In 2018, American border control included a deliberate decision to separate children from their families. In my view, this constitutes torture of parents and children. I find it hard to overlook that.

My father was a great physicist, but he was also a very emotional guy who loved children. At church, when kids fussed and uptight parishioners came out of church complaining, he would smile and respond. His one-liner was that there were very few sounds in the world more delightful than the sound of *someone else's* child misbehaving. Don't misunderstand: he wasn't being cruel. He made people laugh instead of complaining to the pastor and making life hard for struggling parents. He carved out space in church for normal human life. That was his one-liner; but if you gave him a minute, he talked about evolution. He said that human beings are hard-wired to respond to the sounds a child in distress – and they have to be like that, because when a society stops protecting children, it disappears. Evolution selects for people who protect their young.

What about people who are cruel to children? Their families will die out eventually, but what about right now? We must protect the child as well as we can, as fast as we can: nothing on earth matters more. We must prosecute child abuse: nothing on earth matters more. And if child abusers take power, get them out. Nothing on earth matters more!

In his novel about Cromwell's genocidal campaign, *Seek the Fair Land*, Walter Macken has a vignette of a young soldier trying to learn to be brutal. He's been told to kill babies: "from nits come lice." He repeats the mantra, but can't persuade himself it's true. He's too human. What about us?

American policy at the border was not an accident. It was driven, in part, by Stephen Miller, a Cromwell wannabe. Miller is the architect of savage anti-migrant policies spewing from the White House. To understand him, start with a book he likes and promotes: the appallingly brutal French novel, *The Camp of the Saints*, by Jean Raspail, about brown immigrants threatening to over-run Europe. Raspail's brown immigrants are all about excrement. They leave it in the streets; it matches their skin color; and their leader plays with it and eats it. The book even returns to the KKK notion that of course these people of excrement like to rape white girls. The book is disgusting beyond belief. Get it clear in your head: the Trump advisor who devised Trump's anti-immigration policies reads, believes, and promotes horrifying garbage.

When thousands of children were separated from their parents at the border, it wasn't an accident; it was a message from the White House to the people of excrement (Miller's view, not mine). Was this appalling brutality done in your name?

When children are locked in cages, and sit in their own mess crying, it's not an accident; it's a message from the White House, to the people of excrement (Miller's view, not mine) who might think about going north when they flee from gangs. Do you endorse this message?

#30: Feeding the forces that feed the fire

Can I ask a question, just one pro-lifer to another? Why do you think we have abortion in America?

We need books and conferences and all manner of scholarly work to answer properly. But may I, for a moment, explain my view; then you tell me yours. It seems to me that the major social forces leading to abortion are misogyny, eugenics, and racism.

Misogyny. When women are oppressed, and cry out for freedom and lash out to protect themselves, it would be nice if they hit the men who abuse. But that's not always what happens. Often, when a woman is abused, the abuser's child pays the price. Often, a woman shows up at an abortion clinic to get rid of the ball-and-chain that threatens to shackle her permanently, to make her serve some reeking rotten bully for the rest of her life. She wants to get rid of that man, and everything that he has done to her.

When the President brags that he can shove his hand between a woman's legs if he wants to, and when he insults women about their looks, that's not just rude and immature behavior. It's murderous. When a man hits a woman, he may kill a child – not today, but soon enough.

Eugenics. This ideology of arrogance is a massive force, with tentacles, but for the moment I'm focusing on its simplest detail: identifying and getting rid of the weak. For almost a century, geneticists have promised that they can engineer an *improved* human race. Their progress on *improvements* isn't obvious to me. But what they have done very efficiently is to kill. They can identify problems and challenges before birth, and kill them off. Down syndrome is the clearest case: it's easy to identify during pregnancy, and the majority of children detected in utero with this syndrome are dispatched – about two thirds of the Down Syndrome kids found here in the United States, and higher rates elsewhere, up to 98 percent in Iceland.

So when Trump mocks a man with a disability, and when his administration assumes that everyone agrees that we want to keep out immigrants who might need medical care, this attitude is not just rude and crude. It steepens a slide toward death. Trump didn't kill the reporter he mocked – but others later will apply the lesson, and kill babies to avoid embarrassment.

Racism: Since the end of World War II, the United States has promoted eugenic abortion overseas, particularly after the racist ideas in NSSM-200 became policy in 1975. But even within our country, the number of abortions among blacks is far higher than among whites (on a per capita basis). And recall the welfare reforms in the 1990s. They included a "family cap," pressure on poor women – often black – not to have children on welfare. Some pro-lifers opposed this deliberate governmentally devised pressure to avoid birth, because avoiding birth often means abortion. Some, but not all. Racist oppression is a force pushing toward abortion.

Pro-life Republicans oppose an abortion on the day that a child is scheduled to die. Good! Truly wonderful! But pro-life Democrats – and in fact, just about all Democrats – oppose the forces that lead up to that day of lethal violence.

Part IV: The Seamless Garment

My thinking about life and the world and reality was shaped by Vatican II. The Council worked to develop a clear and coherent picture based on the Gospel. The Council taught me to embrace the immense value of consistency. Struggling to follow the Council, I became a peace activist, then a pro-life activist. In my view, the "seamless garment" idea is obvious, fundamental, necessary.

From my perspective, it's appalling that pro-lifers still oppose the idea, still repeat the same mindless nonsense, still insist that "not all issues have the same importance." Sure, good, hierarchies of values – but so what? If I agree not to be a mass murderer, is it okay to be a serial rapist? What kind of monstrous "thinking" is that?

I worked with some of the original proponents of the seamless garment. Perhaps I can persuade some pro-lifers to listen, to respond to the real thing and not to the caricature in their echo chamber.

Permit me to offer six vignettes and observations.

#31: Seamless garment: context clarifies

Is abortion like war, or like sex? People's views vary. To figure out what someone thinks about that question, you can't be content to listen only to what people *say* to answer this question; you also have to listen when they aren't answering directly, when they drop hints. Context clarifies.

In his immense love, God gave me the opportunity to teach English literature for a dozen years. It was a joy, getting up mornings *not* trying to figure out how to transform the world, but just planning how to bring together two of the joys of my life – great literature and wacky teenagers. During those happy years, there was a detail that proved delightful year after year. When I taught students how to read Shakespeare, I used material from the Folger Shakespeare Library, including a method for examining how a great writer adds meaning to a word. I had my students collect every use of some particularly pregnant word in a play, and note how the word grew in meaning and impact from one use to the next. In *Macbeth*, for example, Shakespeare uses the word "blood" to refer to the work of a warrior but also of a murderer, to nobility but also to guilt, to life but also to death, to kinship but also to treachery, to cruelty but also to love, and so on. We read Shakespeare because his works are – like reality – full of startling complexity.

Human speech, like human life, is almost never simple. To understand anything that matters, you must wrestle with apparent contradictions. You must learn to be comfortable with paradox. And to grasp meaning confidently, you need to scrutinize context.

Context explains. To understand what someone means, listen and listen and watch.

Pro-lifers say that abortion is about taking life. It is the destruction of an innocent person.

Pro-choicers say that abortion is about sex. Some sexual

transactions go awry, and you need to be able to back away from mistakes.

So there's a difference about the meaning of the word, and about the meaning of the act.

Do pro-lifers mean what they say? Listen for more than the bumper-sticker sloganeering, the well-trained regurgitation. Watch attentively! Pro-lifers insist that abortion is about life, not about sex. But then, when they talk a little more, it turns out they care about abortion *and birth control*, abortion *and "sodomy,"* abortion *and sexual purity*. Context reveals: regardless of their claim to the contrary, many pro-lifers talk about abortion *and sexual sins*, not about abortion *and death*.

In fact, in recent years, many pro-lifers have made an odd link. Many pro-lifers hate abortion – and demand access to guns. I'm not opposed to the Second Amendment; I'm just saying that's a very strange and interesting link. These pro-lifers have fire in their bellies, but they aren't fanatically opposed to violence.

There are important exceptions. For generations, the leadership of the Catholic Church has opposed abortion, but not the same way as other mainstream pro-life leaders. When the Church's leaders talk about abortion – in Vatican II or social justice documents, or in Pope St. John Paul II's encyclical *The Gospel of Life* – they also talk about war and capital punishment and torture.

Many pro-life leaders denounce this "seamless garment" approach. "Not all issues are the same," they fuss. "There are priorities." But the seamless garment approach has many advantages. For one thing, when you listen to the bishops, it's clear that they're talking about abortion and death, not abortion and sex.

Context clarifies.

#32: Three bits of bio

In the 1970s, when I was finding my way in the pro-life movement, I was involved in some nonviolent action in Connecticut. I did some cross-fertilization: I was arrested at Electric Boat, protesting against nuclear weapons, and I was arrested a few miles away, at Norwich Planned Parenthood, acting against abortion.

When I was organizing the pro-life sit-in, we had several meetings for prayer and meditation at the home of an engineer at Electric Boat. He and I were aware of each other's views, but we worked together without difficulty, with mutual respect. My friend was later unemployed for a time, and then offered a new job, building nuclear weapons platforms again; and he called me to talk about the moral issues involved in his job. He disagreed with me, and he took the job; but he did want to understand my view.

When I engaged in the anti-nuke sit-in, there were 16 of us arrested at the entrance to Electric Boat. Of the 16 peace activists, 14 were pro-life with some involvement in the charismatic renewal. So much for stereotypes.

There was tension between peace activists and pro-life activists, for sure. But it wasn't anywhere near as sharp and bitter then as it is today.

Still, in 1978 or 1979, the New England Catholic Peace Fellowship had a meeting in Amherst. It was an uproarious event. Charlie McCarthy was there, wild-eyed, urging that we meet to pray and plan at 3 AM, when people are more open to spiritual insights, because all of our mental cues are different in the dead of night. Cool idea.

I made a presentation on pro-life nonviolence – not for a couple of outsiders whispering at the edge of a room, but in a regular scheduled workshop. Imagine.

Fr. Dan Berrigan, S.J., gave the keynote address, entitled "War is abortion and abortion is war." One of the points he made was that the abortion struggle might wake us up. The threat of nuclear weapon is often cerebral (except for the Japanese). But abortion is immediate, right in front of us – and so it might get into our hearts and change something in us, he said, "because it's so personally maiming."

At lunch, a number of women came in to confront us. They lined up along a wall and chanted pro-choice slogans. It was a strange kind of a sit-in, peace activists protesting against Berrigan. They respected him, but they were shocked that he would participate in an event like this – especially since there was someone at the conference recruiting for "anti-choice" activity. That would be me, of course. The loudest critic was someone I knew a bit; we had met and chatted during the protest and civil disobedience at Electric Boat. The women came in angry, looking for a confrontation; but there were so many warm friendships tying people together that the anger couldn't get traction, and it just dissolved slowly.

As far as I could tell, everyone in that room had some degree of respect for everyone else. Everyone in that room was committed to listening, to learning, to welcoming, to loving.

When the women were speaking, Berrigan had his head back a little, eyebrows way up and his eyes wide, mouth shut tight: he was in listening mode. It can't have been fun being attacked by friends, but he just looked like a student absorbing a complicated lesson. I saw that same expression in his cameo appearance in the movie *The Mission*.

I am not like Fr. Dan Berrigan. But I try.

#33: Gordon Zahn's insight

In 1976, the pro-life movement in Massachusetts was congenial to leftie liberal Democrats. Ellen McCormack, a lifelong Democrat and a pro-life activist, ran for president that year, and got on the primary ballot in Massachusetts and Vermont (and elsewhere?). Dr. Mildred Jefferson, the first black woman to graduate from Harvard Medical School, was president of National Right to Life Committee; she lived on Beacon Hill in Boston. I think she was a Republican, but she worked comfortably with anyone who enjoyed dancing. In Cambridge, the most visible pro-life activist was Ignatius O'Connor, from the Catholic Worker House.

The leader of this proudly diverse pro-life movement in the commonwealth was Dr. Joseph Stanton. Stanton was trained at Yale Medical School (but that's okay – his father went to Harvard). And when he found an anti-war activist from Harvard stumbling around the edges of the movement, his eyes lit up. He had a book that I had to read, right away. It was written by his friend Gordon Zahn, a professor of sociology at the University of Massachusetts (Boston), who had been a conscientious objector during World War II. So I read *In Solitary Witness: the Life and Death of Franz Jägerstätter*.

Jägerstätter was beheaded in Berlin on August 9, 1943, for refusing induction into the army of the Third Reich. He had discussed his decision with his parish priest and his bishop; they counseled moderation – that is, cooperation. But he refused, and paid the price. Zahn wrote his story, trying to understand the roots of this courage. What he found was that Jägerstätter fathered a child, and did not marry the mother, but did support the child for the rest of his life. This personal confrontation with responsibility transformed a rough-and-tumble troublemaker into a devout Catholic, utterly opposed to abortion and Nazism.

Zahn's book had a huge impact on me, and so I was deeply flattered when he sought me out in the mid-1980s to talk about a book he was planning. He wanted to write about three peace activists whose choice of life rather than abortion had been transformative: Franz Jägerstätter, Dorothy Day, and John Leary.

Dorothy Day is well known; John Leary is not. John was a

Harvard graduate, a few years behind me. He and my sister Lucy were arrested together in pro-life nonviolent actions a number of times. He was a co-founder of the Prolife Nonviolent Action Project, which sparked sit-ins at abortion clinics in all 50 states in the late 1970s. He lived with the Catholic Worker community in Boston, and was a recognized peace activist. He was a devout Catholic, joyful and easy to approach but never shy about his desire to pray. He was quiet and calm, but deeply inspiring. He died young with no obvious accomplishments, but when the Catholic Student Center at Harvard expanded, Jana Kiely (wife of the Master of Adams House) urged that the new building be named for him. (Didn't happen.) Anyway, Zahn was among John's admirers.

In the 1980s, pro-life activists had an annual discussion about scheduling nonviolent action in August: should we have a sit-in on August 9 or August 14 – Jägerstätter's feast day or St. Maximilian Kolbe's?

That's a glimpse from the pro-life movement a generation ago. Times have changed, but that part of our history matters. Perhaps we should retrieve it.

#34: Lessons from Juli Loesch

Juli Loesch (Wiley), the founder of Prolifers for Survival and a pioneer of the seamless garment approach, had a huge impact on me.

"Birds fly better with two wings, a right wing and a left wing": that's a clear and catchy phrase, fundamental to my thinking for years – and it's stolen from Juli Loesch. Sometimes, I don't remember where her thought ends and my own thought begins.

"Bridges and walls are similar, both made of bricks, at boundaries. When you build a bridge, you collect the bricks that other people might use to build walls, or to throw at you." This insight is a permanent challenge in my life – and it's from Juli.

I find a deep joy in it when people quote me without knowing it, using my own words to challenge me: I learned that from Juli Loesch.

My kitchen used to have a small room or large pantry attached; we made it a prayer room for some years, but then it was a bedroom for Juli for some months. It remains a door to joy.

She founded Prolifers for Survival in 1979. She had been out speaking about peace, against nukes – and she had listened enough that she realized that peace activists and pro-lifers were using the same texts from Scripture to make their arguments. Having seen the connections, she went to work building a national network of people who were pro-life and pro-peace – anti-abortion and anti-war. Cardinal Bernardin's "seamless garment" speech was in 1983, four years after she started building her network. It baffles me that people talking about the seamless garment idea don't refer to her work. She traveled across the country – by humble grimy bus, speaking to people in church halls and living rooms, a dozen at a time, or even one at a time – building a network, making connections between the left and right, between peace activists and pro-life activists.

Dan Berrigan got arrested sitting in the door of an abortion clinic – at the end of a conference organized by Juli Loesch and her ragtag bunch of followers. It was Juli's Prolifers for Survival that provided Dan with the opportunity to act publicly against abortion.

I met Juli at the March for Life, probably in 1979; she was leafletting about peace and life links, and I was recruiting for nonviolent action. We hit it off, and cooperated for the next decade. I was the editor of her newsletter, *P.S.*, for a couple of years.

From my perspective, the greatest treasure in her work was her deep abiding joy. The topics she addressed were grim – slaughter in Hiroshima and Nagasaki, slaughter in abortion clinics. She was alone often, out collecting the bricks for bridges one by one. But she prayed regularly, read Scripture, stuck with the Rosary – and radiated joy. She was fun, funny, unpredictable, unquenchable, humble, and tenacious – a living joyful mystery.

She and I drifted apart some years ago, and I don't pretend to understand her thinking now, but I owe her a great deal. I learned from the best.

#35: "Querida Amazonia!"

Pope Francis wrote a fascinating letter about the transformation of the Amazon Basin, the core of South America, "the beloved region of the Amazon." He says the region enriches the world, and that we should cherish it. Many pro-life leaders responded to the Pope's initiative with stunning ignorance and arrogance.

Consider what the Pope wrote, and the response.

The Amazon Basin includes a vast region that wasn't much developed – meaning, made to produce cash – until recently. But now the region is being transformed by loggers and planters. This rape of the land enriches a few investors, not the people who have lived there for centuries. It's barbaric orc-work.

The rape of the land threatens to obliterate over 300 cultures, societies with their own ways of life, and their own languages, living quietly by themselves deep in the jungle.

What happens when you wipe out a culture?

Many of the people die, but not all. Some are driven into cities, uprooted and homeless and desperate. In this social devastation, some become beggars, driven into drug addiction and prostitution.

And then some seek abortion.

The whole situation weighs on the Pope's heart. But some pro-lifers ignore the Latin American Pope's concerns, and question his priorities. They say …

The ecological assault is not a pro-life concern.
The destruction of the rain forest is not a pro-life concern.
The loss of oxygen-producing plants is not a pro-life concern.
The loss of species is not a pro-life concern.
The greed of the developers is not a pro-life concern.
The threat of genocide is not a pro-life concern.
The extinction of cultures is not a pro-life concern.
The displacement of people into cities is not a pro-life concern.
Beggars are not a pro-life concern.
Drug addiction is not a pro-life concern.
Pushing desperate women into prostitution: pro-lifers start to rumble unhappily, but this still isn't exactly a pro-life concern.

Women trapped in prostitution show up at abortion clinics. What a shock. And finally, pro-lifers sit up and take notice.

The President of Brazil, Jair Bolsonaro, supports the rape of the Amazon including genocide, but he opposes abortion – and many pro-lifers in the United States applaud his stand.

But abortion has roots. If you feed the roots, you own the fruits.

If you don't care when people are driven out of the forest into the cities, what do you have to offer them? Where were you when their cultures were obliterated, their homes destroyed, the land stolen?

Pope Francis wrote about this, in *Querida Amazonia*. Pro-life leaders didn't notice when the Pope talked about genocide; instead, they fussed about the possibility of women deacons. They didn't pretend to care when the fragile cultures of the area were demeaned; in fact, they applauded when fiery critic of Vatican II threw an Amazon artifact – a statue of Pachamama – into the Tiber River. They sided with the rich who destroyed the land for profit. And then they demanded self-righteously that people sit up and listen to their words of praise for Bolsonaro, the "pro-life" president of Brazil.

What is wrong with these people?

Genocide isn't brand new. Thomas Malthus wrote his murderous essay about population control in 1798, reacting to the appearance of the Highlanders who were driven off their land in the Scottish mountains and then showed up in English cities. Their skills – their whole proud way of life – was tied to the rough mountains, and was not good preparation for city life; they were despised as ignorant beggars, producing ignorant beggar babies. So the genocide in Scottish Highlands led to Malthusian despair, for generations. And the rape of the Amazon is another chapter in the Malthusian story.

Me: I oppose abortion, and its roots. *And its roots!* The fruit and the root are inseparable, like a seamless garment.

I stand with Francis.

#36: The Bomb

The fundamental assertion of the pro-life movement is that unborn children are members of the human family. If you accept that idea, then abortion in the past five decades or so has been the deadliest assault on humanity in history. About a quarter or even a third of the people conceived since 1968 have died of abortion. Starvation, disease, warfare – nothing compares to the abortion rate. The only thing that could take more lives would be a world war with nukes.

I understand clearly that most people do not consider unborn children to be fully human, members of the human family, entitled to all the protections that everyone else claims as a right. I understand clearly that women made pregnant without their planning such an event often feel trapped, and that uncountable millions of people are convinced that protecting women from abuse and entrapment requires access to abortion. I understand that, and I respect the people who hold this view. But that's not my view; I think unborn children are my brothers and sisters. And I accept the idea that the only thing that could be bloodier is nuclear war.

This perception of abortion drives many pro-lifers to accept just about any craziness erupting from President Trump. Fix the worst, first. I understand that too. But I reject it, for a list of reasons – including that Trump is open to the only violence that could be worse. Since Hiroshima and Nagasaki, every American president has expressed horror about nuclear warfare, and has taken steps to make sure The Bomb is never used again – every president until Trump.

The first time Trump spoke at the United Nations in New York, he threatened to use nukes (9/19/2017).

He threatened to bomb North Korea, with nukes. (9/19/2017 was one time among several).

He threatened to bomb Iran, with nukes (6/23/2019).

When he was a candidate, he said that the military would do what he told them to do, even if they considered his orders to be immoral. He was talking about talking about torture when he said that, but it also applies to bombing civilians, or bombing nations that do not pose a threat to our existence.

He recommended that more nations join the club, get their own nukes. If North Korea has nukes, Japan should get some too (4/3/2016).

One fundamental problem with nukes is that they kill civilians. But Trump said that fighting terrorists requires killing family members (12/2/2015).

For a couple of years, Trump had serious and thoughtful people advising him, making sure he didn't make silly little mistakes like starting a nuclear war. But those people are gone, and now he's surrounded with toadies. He could use a nuke tomorrow.

"Use a nuke." Does that mean press the button and destroy a city, or does it include threats? If someone backs off because you pulled out a gun, did you "use" that gun? Of course you used it. Trump has already used nukes, just not completely.

In my view, there's only one thing more destructive than abortion. And Trump does it. And most pro-lifers don't even notice.

Part V: Population Control

The driving force for abortion, globally, is population control. That's not what's on the minds of women and couples who show up at abortion clinics, but it is a huge part of the motivation for the people who build the clinics and run the industry.

The eugenics movement in the 20th and 21st centuries, aiming to construct a new and improved human race, has four parts. There's "more from the fit," via (1) genetic engineering supported by the new and growing discipline called (2) "bioethics." And there's "less from the unfit," via (3) population control supported by (4) immigration restrictions. (Quick fix: of course bioethics offers much good! But its roots are in eugenics.)

From a eugenic and white supremacist perspective, population control isn't all that important within America. Most Americans are white, so from a eugenics perspective it's okay if they have lots of kids (unless they're "feeble-minded").

Population control is far more visible in Africa, Asia and Latin America than here. There's lots of white money from American and Europe available for programs designed to reduce population there.

The nitty-gritty of population control includes contraception, sterilization, and abortion. Some programs are based on the users' choice; some are based on coercion. But most are based on a hybrid – not openly and physically coercive, but not honest choice either. The eugenicists in the 1950s called it "unconscious voluntary selection." Let that phrase roll around in your head a minute: Orwell would be proud. It's propaganda, manipulation.

(For more, see The Roots of Racism and Abortion.)

Permit me to offer one vignette and three notes regarding population control.

#37: The giant accountant

In 1986, Bill O'Reilly – an accountant, not the TV celebrity – was invited to Bangladesh to audit the Bank of Bangladesh. At that time, O'Reilly worked alone, in a small office in Bethesda; but he had credentials. During the Kennedy administration, he had run the accounting department for the US Post Office. But more pertinent for Bangladesh, Bill's career included an investigation of the finances of New York City, which concluded with a controversial declaration that the city was bankrupt. He was very modest, but he was a serious guy.

When he accepted the Bangladesh job, Bill planned a six-week trip; but he finished his work there much faster than that. When he got there, it only took a day or two to figure out his job. The Bank was not independent; it was government-controlled. And it was bankrupt. Everyone knew it, but nobody could say it out loud. They hired him, an outside expert, to say it out loud. So he said it out loud – and then he had almost the whole six weeks left to explore a wonderful although poverty-stricken country.

Pro-lifers can make very odd tourists. Bill poked around here and there, and discovered that the World Bank was preparing a development loan for Bangladesh, with a long list of much-needed projects for a variety of social services, including 400 maternal and child health clinics. But the clinics all included a "menstrual regulation" component.

Bangladesh was a Muslim nation, and abortion was illegal. But the plan was to offer help for women whose menstrual cycle became irregular. If a woman realized that she hadn't menstruated for six weeks or longer, and that there might be some complication, she could visit a clinic for a simple procedure that would restore a regular flow. I guess that sounds innocent, if you're ignorant. In plainer terms, skipping the euphemisms and the disguise, the World Bank was about to build 400 abortion clinics, despite the anti-abortion laws of the land.

Bill returned to the United States and wrote it up. He pulled me into his project, and I helped him write his pamphlet, "Deadly Neo-Colonialism." Fr. Paul Marx at Human Life International funded publication. Armed with a clear and concise explanation of the violent fraud, O'Reilly lobbied the World Bank to cancel the project. It was too late to alter it; the loan was facing an up-or-down vote, without amendments. The Bank is supposed to be lobby-proof, but Bill didn't know that, so he lobbied – and succeeded. The Bank didn't cancel the project, but did add a side agreement, affirming that none of the funds in the loan would be used for abortion, under any name.

Bill (with a little help) closed 400 abortion clinics. I do not know for sure what happened subsequently; but if his work survived, it is possible that approximately 15% of the people alive in Bangladesh today owe their lives in part to this gentle giant, this obscure accountant.

Not long after this, a great feminist opponent of coercive population control, Betsy Hartmann, wrote a masterful dissection of Western interference (*Reproductive Rights and Wrongs: The Global Politics of Population Control*), citing her experience in Bangladesh, and denouncing the sterilization campaign there. She made reference to the startling support she got from a couple of "rightwingers," meaning Bill and me. We wrote to explain that we were pro-life *Democrats*, and we joked that we would sue her if she insulted us and impugned our reputations in this way again. I don't know whether she laughed, but she fixed the error.

#38: A coopted movement: consider Hungary

In 2000, I attended a meeting of the International Association of Bioethics, in London. Daniel Wikler, a former president of the IAB, was just releasing his new book about the differences between the old destructive eugenics and the new hopeful eugenics. He had announced his plan for the book at a meeting in 1996, and I had argued with him about it, but he ignored my criticisms. The book argues that the old eugenics was bloody: think Hitler. But, he argues, the *new* eugenics can be helpful: think babies with improved genes. The problem is, the new eugenics includes coercive abortion in national population control programs – anti-life, anti-choice, anti-child, anti-woman, government-run. Wikler's book was applauded by coercive Chinese family planners. Eugenics is *not* reformed; it remains a massively bloody utopian nightmare.

The thing that matters here is that a murderous eugenics campaign can include opposition to abortion, can include a sustained push to protect babies and births and marriages and fatherhood and motherhood and family life – in wellborn wealthy educated *white* communities. A serious and organized eugenic push can cooperate with a pro-life movement – in *white* nations. The flip side of "less from the unfit" is "more from the fit" – two sides of as single coin. Hitler was for abortion for Jews but against abortion for Aryans. So in some settings, he was "pro-life" (if you accept that word as a synonym for opposing abortion).

Can that happen again? Of course! Look at Hungary, poor bloodied Hungary! And look at the enthusiasm among American pro-lifers about Hungary's brave new efforts!

God have mercy on Hungary, a proud but haunted nation. It was smashed up the Nazis, recovered briefly and then was smashed up by the Soviets, recovered briefly and then was smashed up again by a rightwing dictatorship.

My best friend in grade school was Hungarian. His father, Aladar Szegedy-Maszak, was the Hungarian ambassador to the United States after World War II. He was in a Nazi concentration camp, and then was exiled by the Communists. I remember him as a man of immense dignity, visibly tortured by memories.

Hungary today is working hard to raise its birthrate, and also to keep out non-whites. It has a happy-happy sweet and encouraging pro-birth national policy, balanced with a savagely inhospitable anti-Muslim border policy.

In the greatest refugee crisis since World War II, much of Europe has been hospitable – including Sweden, Germany, France, and the UK. But some nations have refused to help refugees – including Poland, Slovakia, the Czech Republic, and Hungary. In 2018, Hungary's ruling party, Fidesz, tightened its grip on the nation's parliament by running a single-issue campaign: anti-immigrant.

The last national census in Hungary (in 2011) found 5,579 Muslims, less than a tenth of a percent of the nation. You have to be paranoid to see that as a grave threat.

Faced with a steep population decline, the Prime Minister, Viktor Orban, supports incentives for marriage and births, including tax breaks, mortgage repayments, car purchase subsidies, payments to care for grandparents, and grants to pro-life organizations. The 2012 Hungarian constitution states that life will be protected from conception. Interestingly, that has not ended access to abortion – yet.

Orban is determined to avoid "an exchange of populations, to replace the population of Europeans with others." "Others": that means non-white, especially Muslims from the Middle East.

Orban is explicit about the immigration-abortion link. His slogan: "Procreation, not immigration." The Trump administration applauds this manipulative brutality.

It makes me sick to say it, but the pro-life movement is full of people who applaud Orban's murderous eugenics program. They hold it up as a model.

#39: Refugees and abortion

Understanding the bloody impact of America's immigration restrictions requires a little history. Let me race through a century – five vignettes in five paragraphs – to make a point.

First, when eugenicists gained power in America in the 1920s, they launched three legislative initiatives. They banned miscegenation ("inter-racial" marriage), and they began compulsory sterilization of the "feeble-minded," and they restricted immigration. Our immigration laws today are reforms of those eugenic and racist laws. Restricting immigration does not rid the world of unwashed and unwanted people, but it does protect the racial purity of a nation. The intent was clear.

Second, the anti-immigration laws here supported Hitler's work in Europe. In 1937, a passenger ship, the St Louis, sailed out of Hamburg, carrying hundreds of Jewish refugees to America. But when the ship arrived here, we refused to permit passengers to disembark. The ship returned to Germany, and most of those people whom we turned away, who had seen the lights of Miami, were killed in death camps. At the Holocaust Museum in Washington, there's a list of passengers who sailed back to Europe to die – killed by our laws which supported Hitler's aims. Restricting immigration here strengthened murderous depopulation measures there.

Third, the Golden Venture incident showed that restricting immigration here can strengthen forced abortion elsewhere. In 1993, a cargo ship, the Golden Venture, ran aground on Long Island. There were 286 Chinese men and women on board; the vessel belonged to "snakeheads," Chinese gangsters who smuggled "illegal aliens." The fugitives were rounded up for deportation. But some of them were pregnant women fleeing from forced abortion, a brutal aspect of China's one-child-only policy. Rep. Chris Smith (R-NJ) and other pro-lifers fought to protect fleeing women and their unborn children. Smith, a member of the House Committee on Foreign Affairs, pushed through legislation to grant asylum to a limited number of refugees from forced abortion or sterilization. The incident forced pro-lifers to consider the links between our border policies and brutality elsewhere; at that time, pro-lifers chose to protect life.

In 1995, a French novel that promoted white supremacy, Jean Raspail's *Camp of the Saints*, was re-published with a cover that appears to be taken from the Golden Venture incident – a rusty ship in the background and poorly dressed non-white people pouring ashore. Today, immigration policy in the Trump administration is often devised and promoted by Stephen Miller, who has been urging people to read this book for years.

In the 1970s, pro-lifers understood population control and resisted it. But there has been a change – a slow change, but broad and deep. Today, pro-life leaders are generally supportive of Trump's anti-immigrant policies, due in some part to the successful propaganda from NumbersUSA, one of the organizations founded by John Tanton, a proponent of global population control. Tanton worked with Planned Parenthood for years, but he considered them slow and inefficient. He went off to build his own groups. NumbersUSA is a propaganda powerhouse that has successfully recruited huge numbers of pro-lifers to support population control. For example, their cute little video about gumballs has been circulating among pro-lifers for years: it's presented as an explanation of immigration, but halfway through it shifts to global population. It's slick and effective – and murderous.

Margaret Sanger recruited feminists into the eugenics movement; Tanton recruits pro-lifers. Successfully.

#40: MAGA versus Pelosi

Pro-life leaders hate to admit it, but they are not making plans to end abortion. It's their desire, but not their plan. In the foreseeable future, they plan to trim, not end. A realistic strategy to end abortion begins with a campaign of nonviolence, but at this time most pro-life leaders are committed to polarization, demonizing their opponents; this is not nonviolence. If the plan is to trim, not end, let's talk about how to trim the most.

Most pro-lifers assume quietly, without much discussion, that reversing *Roe v Wade* will end abortion. I think that's total nonsense; but to make my point, let's assume the Supreme Court does reverse *Roe*. Also, most pro-lifers don't get around to discussing what happens when you try to enforce a law like the one they propose; but to make my point, let's assume the law will be enforced successfully. If we give pro-life leaders everything they want – they get a reversal, and new protective laws, and they even get a third miracle, effective enforcement – what changes?

We get a trim – just 2%, or maybe 3%. America has about 5% of the world's population, and 2-3% of the world's surgical abortions.

2-3%. That's it; that's all. This is about MAGA, Trump's Make *America* Great Again. America helped to start and grow abortion all over the world, but pro-life leaders are aiming – in their wildest dreams – to end abortion *in America only*, which means that they want to protect 2-3% of the babies in danger in the world. Their wildest dream, unprecedented in the history of the world, succeeding with a list of miracles, is a trim, a 2-3% trim.

By contrast, suppose we work with Nancy Pelosi, and get everything she wants but nothing more.

She opposes forced abortion. The statistics on that are really messy! How do you define "force"? But a reasonable ballpark estimate is that 30% of abortion globally is coerced.

My friend John Ryan, a true pro-life hero, insists that we keep in mind that *all* abortion is coercive from the perspective of the unborn child. Noted. But about 30% of abortions include some form of coercion applied to the mother. The worst campaign of forced abortion in the world – indeed the bloodiest chapter in all of human history, in my view as a pro-lifer – is the one-child-only depopulation policy in China. It's been eased a bit, but not erased; it's a two-child-only policy now. It's anti-life and also anti-choice; it's anti-child and also anti-woman. And Pelosi has opposed that policy for decades.

Pro-life leaders are working to trim abortion, not end it. And if you let them trim all they want (all they are currently talking about in their wildest dreams), they will trim 2-3%.

If Pelosi got everything she wanted in her wildest dreams, she would trim abortion 30%.

MAGA pro-lifers, given everything they want, would divide America bitterly and save a million babies' lives each year.

Pelosi, given everything she wants, would unite America and save 15 million babies' lives each year.

I admit that Pelosi, although she is remarkable, can't get complete global cooperation and stop all coercive abortion. But that's where her ideas aim: 30%.

I wish pro-lifers would admit that they won't reverse *Roe* (miracle #1) *and* get protective laws in 50 states (15 more miracles) *and* enforce them successfully (50 more miracles). But their ideas, their most ambitious ideas – MAGA to the max, with 66 miracles – would trim 2%, maybe 3%.

For the time being, pro-lifers can only hope to trim abortion, not end it. (For now.) So how much of a trim do you want to aim for? 3% or 30%?

So I'm a pro-life Democrat, with a global view.

Part VI: Common Ground and Civility

In our time, we are sorting out an apparent collision involving the right to life and the call to freedom. The values expressed by the two sides in this struggle are not subject to compromise in any simple way. But what is possible, today and always, is a search for common ground, and a civil recognition of the immense human dignity of our opponents.

Permit me to offer several vignettes and three dreams.

#41: "Choice" is not the enemy

I try to listen to the Lord, but sometimes I am thick-headed. It seems to me that the Lord has to say things at least three times before I notice. And so, decades ago, it took three incidents within a few weeks to pry open my reluctant eyes, to see that pro-lifers can and should be ready to cooperate with pro-choicers sometimes.

First incident. A neighbor came to see me, to talk about his teenage daughter's pregnancy. She was still in high school, and neither he nor his wife thought she was ready to be a mother. They were planning to make sure she did the only intelligent thing, as they understood it, as soon as possible. But she didn't want an abortion. And she had asked her dad to go see me to talk about it. I didn't bother making a pro-life argument. I argued that if they weren't pro-life, they should at least be pro-choice.

I don't mean to be dishonest: if the daughter had wanted an abortion, I wouldn't have made that argument. But it was an easier argument to make, and it worked out. The child was born, and today all three generations in that family are pleased about their decision.

Second incident. I was outside the Hillcrest abortion clinic in SE Washington, talking to women and couples approaching the place. There were a dozen or so pro-choice folks outside, blocking my way so I couldn't converse (or "interfere and harass," depending on your point of view). A car pulled into the lot, and a man got out of the driver's seat. He went around to the passenger side, and talked a bit, then shouted a bit, and then wrenched the door open, grabbed the woman sitting there, and pulled her out. She screamed and cried, but he dragged her toward the door. I tried to speak up a bit, although I can't remember what I said. The pro-choice group blocked my way. If either the man or the woman tussling their way to the door noticed anything from the sidewalk, they probably heard just noise. The man won: he dragged her inside. I don't know anything more about their story; as far as I know they were there for a few hours, long enough to complete her planned procedure.

But when that door shut and they were inside, I lost it, and shouted for a few minutes, denouncing the people who blocked me. Skipping the profanity, I called them hypocrites. How could they dare to call themselves "pro-choice," when they watched a man drag a woman inside – physically, no metaphor here – and they had nothing to say about it. They took the man's side against the woman's choice. Empty dishonest manybadwords!

Third incident. There was a debate in Congress, about American support for family planning programs overseas. Part of the debate was about coercive abortion: would America support forced abortion? Congress was moving toward funding international family planning, but not coercive programs. In that context, there was a debate about the definition of "coercive." If the Chinese program pushes women toward abortion – without physical coercion, using only financial and social pressure – for example, reducing her wages or benefits, and ostracizing her – is that "coercive"? Pro-lifers wanted a broad definition. But the person who led the fight on the floor of the House to ensure that coercion was defined broadly was a pro-choice Congresswoman, Nancy Pelosi. She fought against American funding of coercive abortion, defined broadly, and she prevailed.

Three times in a few weeks, the strongest pro-life argument was a pro-choice argument. The Lord of creation speaks through reality. So I can't demonize pro-choicers; they aren't the enemy. The real struggle is more complicated than that.

#42: One small common ground effort

The search for common ground is partly a history of frauds. We got our common ground, and they got theirs. Nonetheless, I'm committed to the search. There are frauds, but there are also valuable insights. And even without conceptual breakthroughs, civility is immensely valuable, always.

The pro-choice proffer of common ground often includes sex education, contraception, and concern about teen pregnancy. I don't think this goes very far. Planned Parenthood considers sexual activity outside marriage to be normal, considers pregnancy a common hazard, and sometimes considers birth a disaster. But Catholics consider sexual activity outside marriage a common hazard, considers pregnancy a blessing, and birth a cause for joy. There's *not* a lot of common ground there.

The pro-life proffer has sometimes included pregnancy aid, opposition to pornography, and opposition to infanticide. But the devil is in the details: will pregnancy aid include ultrasound? Can you define pornography? Infanticide: isn't this a transparent slippery slope argument?

But perhaps we can cooperate in opposing forced abortion – pro-lifers oppose it because it's abortion and pro-choicers oppose it because it's forced.

A search for common ground is a fraud if it unites one side and divides the other. I am not certain that resisting coercive abortion passes that test for fraud. That is, I think the proponents of abortion are a coalition of feminists and eugenicists. It seems to me that there are millions of people who identify themselves as pro-choice who support coercive abortion, and I think it will weaken the pro-choicers to opt for honesty and separate themselves from population control advocates. So do I really want to find common ground, or do I want to divide the opposition? To be honest, I want to do both – and I leave it to pro-choicers to decide who they are and whether this can work.

There's some encouraging history. The two sides have sometimes cooperated in opposition to forced abortion.

Some years ago, I asked a pro-choice friend if she would picket the Chinese embassy with me, because the Chinese family planning policy at that time permitted one child only per family. That policy was anti-life and also anti-choice, so perhaps we could picket together. She agreed, with several stipulations: this was a one-time event, not the beginning of something; and we would be brief; and we wouldn't advertise; and this was a personal event, not a political act. I agreed, and we picketed.

At that time, the Chinese embassy was on a busy road, Connecticut Avenue at Kalorama Circle, just south of the bridge over Rock Creek. Cars came across the bridge, then turned left a little, making it easy to read our signs on the ride side of the road. My sign said, "Pro-lifers oppose forced abortion in China," and hers said, "Pro-choicers oppose forced abortion in China."

Some people coming around the curve saw me and started to give me the finger – then saw her, and froze, or brushed away flies, or picked their noses absent-mindedly. Others saw her and started to shake their fists – then saw me and froze, scratched their ears, or patted their bald heads. People eating sandwiches stopped chewing and stared. Eyes popped, mouths dropped. No one went by without registering shock. Cognitive dissonance run amok!

She had said this was to be a personal event, not political – just to see how it felt. It felt good.

#43: Simple civility matters

Let me offer two quick incidents.

First incident

In 1984 (approx), three pro-lifers entered the procedure room of the Planned Parenthood clinic in Silver Spring, and made ourselves comfortable. As long as we were there, no one would die.

We considered our action to be a nonviolent intervention, protecting unborn children from death and protecting women from exploitation. The staff at the facility considered our action to be an invasion – of their patients' privacy, and also of Planned Parenthood's private property.

The person in charge there, an assistant administrator named Debbie Y– , ordered us to leave, and argued with us a bit. When it became clear that we weren't going to leave voluntarily, she called the cops. And their view was simple: intervention or invasion, it was illegal. They arrested us.

After we were arrested and handcuffed, we lay on the floor awhile waiting for transportation. Debbie saw me, handcuffed and a little uncomfortable, and got me a pillow. I was okay; I didn't need a pillow. And what was at stake was far more significant than some healthy guy's complete comfort. Still, what she did was kind – and it was kindness to an opponent. In fact, I guess we were "enemies": she was kind to an enemy. I admired her civility, and I still treasure the memory. That pillow was emphatically not just a pillow; it included a brief glimpse of her heart.

That was 35 years ago; if I bumped into her, I wouldn't recognize her. But I still think of her often – not every day, but every month – and I pray that I will be like her, in some ways.

Second incident

In a common ground initiative, I got to know a thoughtful woman who ran an abortion clinic. When we trusted each other enough to ask questions, I asked her how she could do such destructive work. She said she had been abused by her husband. No, no, I said, please don't change the topic; please explain why you do this. She said her husband had abused her. I asked and she answered like that over and over and over, maybe a dozen times. And then very slowly I figured out that she wasn't changing the topic. She was answering my question precisely. I didn't recognize the answer because I was ignorant. She was patient with me, and I got it eventually, because (1) I trusted her and (2) she was patient.

I would add a few words to make her answer clearer, something like: "I swore I would always help women who felt trapped by abusive men – always, no matter what." But those are my words, not hers; I'm guessing. I disagree with her; I think loyalty has limits. But I think I understand her at least dimly, and I admire her.

What drives her, if I understand it, isn't really logical, but it is (1) completely understandable and (2) common. So people who are interested in reality will adjust to her view. And that means, in part, grasping the fact that abusing women kills children. So, pro-life friends: when you see someone abusing a woman, see also a dead baby, and respond accordingly.

She transformed the way I understand pro-life work. As Yogi Berra could have said: you hear a lot of things by listening.

#44: Together against eugenic abortion

Can pro-lifers and pro-choicers agree on one small step to eliminate or minimize eugenic abortions due to a powerful medication?

There are about five thousand Accutane abortions annually. That's a soft figure, an extrapolation from limited studies in Canada a decade ago. And the name "Accutane" is not in use anymore; that's the original brand name for isotretinoin, no longer made by the original manufacturer but still available as a generic drug. It's the treatment of last resort for acne, and it's powerful. But it causes birth defects, often enough that the FDA requires physicians who prescribe it to make sure their female patients are using birth control. But then, when something goes wrong, about 90% of the women who find themselves pregnant while taking Accutane choose abortion.

Acne isn't a joke: it scars your face, and it scars your psyche. And Accutane works well. But what about these associated abortions?

If nothing else comes from it, Accutane abortions should at least lead to a respectful discussion between pro-lifers and pro-choicers. Today, most pro-life leaders are tied tightly to the Republican party, which generally opposes government regulation, and most people who identify themselves as pro-choice are more supportive of government regulation. So what will the two sides say about strengthening FDA, so that it can ban Accutane, or at least regulate it more effectively?

There are about five thousand eugenic abortions annually that could be prevented by taking a drug off the market. Will pro-lifers talk about it among themselves, and decide to focus their attention and the attention of the nation on this? Or will they promptly defend the free market, and oppose governmental interference?

The question has curves. In years past, the national leader most likely to strengthen the FDA was a conservative Republican, Sen. Chuck Grassley from Iowa. When he was chair of the Senate committee overseeing the FDA, he took on the drug companies over and over, with determination. He was a conservative, but he was not anti-regulation when lives were at stake. And in his struggles to strengthen the FDA in years past, his opponent, often, was Sen. Ted Kennedy. Unexpected curves.

Suppose most people agree that Accutane has benefits that we simply won't vote to ban, that we won't discard it completely until we find something that treats acne as effectively. Can pro-lifers and pro-choicers work together on an educational campaign focusing on sexually active women upset about acne? Just say no – to Accutane?

Regardless of the state of the law for the time being, can pro-lifers and pro-choicers work together to get at a horror lurking in the background of the Accutane fight? What is this obsession with producing perfect babies? Why in the name of all that is gentle is there such a strong consensus – like 90 percent! – that children with congenital abnormalities should be discarded, if they are found "in time" – that is, before birth? Can we work together to disrupt this horrifying but nearly universal demonic fixation?

Can we, together, reject violence perpetrated for eugenic purposes?

#45: Common ground: study eugenics

I support a search for common ground. Not long ago, many Americans spent the Fourth of July with picnics and food and alcohol and fireworks – but also with speeches or shows recalling the fights and attitudes that Americans share. Together, we embrace the ideas in the Declaration of Independence. Imperfectly but sincerely, we proclaim – together – that some truths are obvious, including that all people are created equal, and that we all have some rights that are ours simply because we are human. Together, we admire the courage and determination of Washington at Valley Forge and the other heroes who made these words come alive with enough vigor that they became the foundation of a nation. We share these ideas and ideals.

We squabble about the American project. Were the Founding Fathers all hypocrites? Does religious liberty embrace Muslims? Does the Bill of Rights give each of us permission to join an unlimited arms race with our neighbors?

The Civil War was about a compromise in our assertion of ideals. While we held slaves, we stated that all men are created equal. So we had to decide, sooner or later, whether we would abandon the ideal and keep our slaves, or hold tight to the ideal and free our slaves. As a nation, we fought a war to settle that question, and the side that held to the ideal of equality prevailed. When we said that we held it to be self-evident that all men are created equal, we meant it, despite our grave shortcomings.

Today in America, we are split again, with growing bitterness, over two versions of this ideal. Like any bitter fight, this one has a list of grievances described differently depending on where you stand. But let me focus on migration and abortion. It seems to me that both sides in the current split are guilty of placing limits on our joint declaration of rights.

One side asserts that rights are given by the state – the united states – not by God, and that our nation doesn't have any obligation to recognize the rights of non-Americans. MAGA! We will make *America* great, not *humanity*; outsiders don't have a "right" to immigrate.

The other side asserts that human rights are indeed held by all humans, regardless of national borders – but what's a human? Embryos aren't people. We have to make a decision, as a society, when we will recognize this growing entity as a member of our society, maybe at birth or maybe whenever the pregnant woman decides she's a mother; but for sure, assert most leaders of the Democratic Party, things that are the size of a mosquito brain, that look like mulberries, aren't human.

To me, it seems strange beyond telling that when you know someone's position on immigration, you can often predict their view on abortion – not always, but often. The partisan split today is about many things, but there's a fiery core: we have different views regarding the rights in our shared Declaration.

I think it would be worthwhile to launch a national exploration of eugenics, the ideology that gave birth to abortion on one side, and race-based immigration restrictions on the other.

Can we cooperate, and is it worthwhile? I note with interest that the Southern Poverty Law Center, which is solidly *pro-choice*, makes extensive use of research done on the American Eugenics Society (renamed the Society for the Study of Social Biology, and now called the Society for Biodemography and Social Biology) – research by a deeply committed *pro-lifer*.

#46: Common ground: help pregnant refugees

I can't help coming back to this simple hope, that Americans can agree to help pregnant refugees and nursing mothers.

There's a temptation, among Republicans, to see a pregnant refugee as a plain old refugee, someone else's problem, one of millions. If you help that woman, the next step is her smelly boyfriend, and then her whole extended family – her village, actually.

There's a temptation, among Democrats, to see pregnancy aid as a fraud, an anti-abortion ploy, an emotion-laden camel's nose under the tent with the whole rightwing world backed up behind it. The next step, if you tolerate that nose, is camel-spit, and then a minute later the big tent becomes a circus.

I understand the fears.

So see the problems, then: you can't help but see them. But see also the person! Face the problems with her, and solve them with her, one by one, as well as you can! Here's a pregnant young woman. She's homeless and running, but she won't be hopeless or helpless anymore if we meet her eye to eye and then act like the human beings we want to be.

At the border, a pregnant woman should be given priority, and provided with food, water, clothing, shelter, telephone, medical care, and advocacy. Can Americans do that, together?

In refugee camps, the United States should cooperate with the UN High Commissioner for Refugees to provide expanded care for pregnant women, including medical care and advocacy. Can Americans do that, together?

Pro-choice advocates may want to argue that if want to help pregnant women, we need to provide abortion as well as pregnancy- and birth-related support. Two responses. First, carrying a child to birth is far more expensive than abortion – literally a thousand times more expensive, $300 versus $300,000. So it's arguably balanced and reasonable – and abortion-neutral – to provide aid for the more expensive choice. Second, adding abortion to a pregnancy aid program would promptly undercut broad support for it.

Immigration advocates might want to argue that the best way to help refugees is simply to provide what they are asking for, what they have a right to: asylum. We should respect the rights of all refugees, not just a slice. I won't argue against that, except to say that when we can't take a full step, it may help to take a half step.

It seems to me that good people on both sides of the national divide want to help pregnant refugees. Perhaps we can't help them, because we can't cooperate across the partisan divide. But it seems to me that this shameful obstacle is among the best reasons for trying: we need to re-establish a habit of cooperating when we can. In a large and complex nation, we want people cooperating with opponents to get something good done. Working together on a good project can help people to see each other in a good light. Cooperation on a limited project will not solve the abortion battles, nor the immigration crisis. But it will help us to stop demonizing each other.

We are divided, but cooperation is still possible. I'm not arguing; don't prove me wrong. I'm inviting: prove me right.

Blessed is she who comes in the name of the Lord.

Books by John Cavanaugh-O'Keefe

My books are in three categories.

strategy

I started Pro-Life Democrat claiming that I have a strategy, and asking whether the current national leaders of the pro-life movement can make the same claim.

My ideas about how to build a culture of life in this century are laid out in two books. One is about pro-life strategy: in my view, the heart of the work must be a campaign of nonviolence. See Emmanuel, Solidarity: God's Act, Our Response. The other is about the forces that drive abortion – found in eugenics. See The Roots of Racism and Abortion: An Exploration of Eugenics

immigration

The great collision in our time, separating Democrats and Republicans with some bitterness and anger, involves different visions of the future, different ideas about the next generation. There are two ways to get new citizens: birth and immigration. And the nation is divided about how to them.

I have written several books addressed primarily to pro-lifers, about immigration. See list below.

works of mercy

One of the underlying disagreements between Democrats and Republicans is about morality and society. Republicans often tie morality tightly to questions of personal life, not social life. Democrats often speak of social evils in ways that Republicans don't understand.

To bridge this gap, I think that it's worthwhile looking carefully at the words of Jesus Christ regarding the "works of mercy."

See Restoring the Works of Mercy.

#47: Pro-life strategy, pro-choice strategy

In 1999, I was fired by a pro-life organization, for a collection of horrors including that I'm a liberal. I was hired by another group, but then fired again after a few months, suspected again of liberalism. Worse: during that year, I spent some time arguing with pro-lifers about how to respond to the murder of Barnett Slepian, an OB/GYN in upstate New York who did abortions. The man suspected (later convicted) of the murder was Jim Kopp. I'd been to jail with Kopp, and he had been a part of a campaign to start pro-life nonviolence in Europe, a campaign that I helped build. Jim fled after the murder, and was on the run for two years. While he was a fugitive, on the FBI's list of most wanted fugitives, I urged pro-lifers across America and in several other countries where he knew pro-lifers to turn him if they saw him. So I was an accused liberal, and also a flagrant rat-fink; I lost a long list of friends that year. My position within the pro-life movement was weaker than ever. So in 2000, I went off to teach high school English for a while.

But before I went off to teach, I wrote two books, one explaining my view of a real pro-life strategy, the other calling for a re-evaluation of our opponents. The first was about nonviolence; the second was about eugenics. I re-published both of them in 2012, and they are available on Amazon or Kindle.

Emmanuel, Solidarity: God's Act, Our Response

Scripture commands us, "Rescue those doomed to die." But how? The book explains a campaign of pro-life nonviolence that I helped to launch. The book has three parts. It begins with a *commonsense* approach: unborn children and women who are facing an unexpected and unwelcome pregnancy need help, and decent people will offer that help, promptly and directly. Second, it explains the reasons from *history* for a specifically nonviolent approach, imitating Gandhi and King and Lech Walesa and Corazon Aquino. And third, it explains how the *teaching of the Catholic Church* supports nonviolent action to protect women and children.

Amazon: $11. Kindle: $3.

The Roots of Racism and Abortion: An Exploitation of Eugenics

Eugenics – what's that and why should I care? It's the Master Race program, the ideology of arrogance. Most people have never heard of it, and most of the people who know the word think it died with Hitler. But all four parts of the movement are functioning fine, stronger than ever. It is astounding that so few people push back against it! Eugenics brought us racism (the academic racism version especially), coercive abortion, abusive genetic engineering, anti-immigration laws – to mention a few. The book argues that it's silly to confront pieces of the eugenics movement one by one without addressing the whole problem. Push back against the whole package! But start by getting a handle on the history and theory of this pseudo-science, the practice of this destructive ideology.

Amazon: $9. Kindle: $3.

#48: Immigration in Scripture and Tradition

In 2012, in Maryland, pro-life activists led the fight against welcoming immigrants. I was appalled; I felt betrayed. So I started working to explain to my colleagues of many years why their drift into xenophobia was completely crazy. I looked at the teaching about immigration in the Old Testament, the New Testament, and Tradition as understood by the Catholic Church.

Old Testament, especially Exodus

When Jesus said, "Welcome strangers," what did he mean? The command was non-trivial; it's one of six about which he said, do this and meet my Father or don't and go to hell. But what does "welcome" mean, and what's a "stranger"?

Okay, find the meaning of two words. To be confident, you want to know where and when the word is used, and what the cultural context is. What Jesus meant should be clear when it's seen within the context of the culture in which he taught – that is, in the Old Testament. So I set out to understand what the Old Testament says about welcoming strangers. I was shocked by what I found: the teaching in the Old Testament is clear, forceful, and abundant. I don't know how I missed it, for decades!

The key texts focus on the principal moral lesson from the Exodus: "Welcome strangers because – remember! – you too once were a stranger in a strange land." The Hebrew word for stranger is "ger," and it means whatever the Hebrews were when they were in Egypt. "Homeless" is a weak translation; a far more accurate translation is "immigrant."

I wrote up what I found in *Strangers: 21 Claims in the Old Testament*. Amazon: $6. Kindle: $3.

New Testament, especially Matthew 25

If I was right that there was teaching about immigration in hundreds of texts in the Old Testament, then it had to be in the

New Testament as well. Is it?

Yes, it's far more abundant in the New Testament. But there's a shift that you have to notice and understand. Moses and Jesus both talked about how to respond to people outside our comfort zones, people who are *other*, people who are *them-not-us*. Moses talked about native-born Hebrews versus strangers; Jesus talked about neighbors versus non-neighbors. So the ways they phrased the questions were not quite identical, but very close. Moses said, when you encounter a stranger, recall our experience in Egypt and use that memory to get inside the experience of the stranger, and then you will know how to respond. Abraham's experience adds that you should welcome strangers because you might thereby meet God. Jesus said, when you encounter someone in need, put yourself in that person's situation and your imagination will guide you to respond appropriately. And he added, when you encounter a stranger, you encounter me.

The Lord's identification with strangers, and his concern for strangers, is everywhere in the New Testament, from the birth narratives right through to the mission to the Gentiles.

I wrote up what I found in *The Persistent Other*. Amazon: $5.50. Kindle: $3.

Patristic Literature and Aquinas

If Scripture, both the Old Testament and the New Testament, contain extraordinarily rich teaching about welcoming immigrants, is it in the teaching of the Church?

I focused on the teaching of eight people, identified as "The Great Fathers" – four Western (Latin) and four Eastern (Greek) – plus St. Benedict and St. Thomas Aquinas. The teaching that I thought I found in Scripture is indeed all throughout the writings of the Fathers and Doctors of the Church.

The Fathers can be intimidating. But if you aren't afraid of Moses and Jesus, why should Jerome and Basil scare you off? Knock them off their pedestals, and listen to what these smart brothers have to say!

Jerome clawed the sky, frustrated about how to persuade Christians to welcome refugees.

Augustine asked his listeners if they were a little jealous of Zacchaeus, who had Jesus as his guest for dinner. Don't be jealous, he says: go grab a refugee, and bring the Lord to dinner!

Patristic literature starts with a lot of men – males, that is – but all the great heroes of Christian hospitality were men *working with women*: Sts. Jerome *and Fabiola*, Sts. Basil *and Macrina*, Sts. Benedict *and Scholastica*, etc. A renewal of hospitality begins with women.

I wrote up what I found in *The Two Stout Monks Myth*. Amazon: $5.50. Kindle: $3.

The Great Eclipse

If there's abundant teaching about immigration in Scripture and Tradition, why isn't it familiar?

I offer two ideas about this odd disappearance, this fantastic obscurancy, this great eclipse. First, the teaching got smudged and fudged when the great teaching tool – the "corporal works of mercy" – drifted away from its roots in Matthew 25. Aquinas noticed the rupture and the drift, and suggested that the teaching tool should be re-attached to the Gospel. But the drift continued, and the idea that hospitality fundamental in Christian life – like, say, truth and justice – got lost.

And second, while the *idea* was obscured, the *practice* was also undermined. During most of the history of the Church, hospitality was understood as the responsibility (and joy) of monks and nuns and clergy, who acted in the name of the Church (and in response to the Lord). That was fine for centuries. But when monastic life was disrupted during the Reformation – most obviously in England, where monasteries were suppressed – the old pattern disappeared, and there was no alternative plan in hand.

I wrote about this in *Knocking at Haven's Door*. Amazon: $6. Kindle: $3.

#49: The works of mercy in the Gospel

One of the strangest details in the strange history of Christianity is what happened to the Lord's teaching about the works of mercy. The Lord's style of teaching seems simple, with folksy parables, but is in fact remarkably (divinely) rich, subject to interpretation on many different levels. What he said taught should be understood on a literal level, and historical and metaphorical and moral and anagogical and spiritual and ... Everything he said is interpreted on many levels, with a single exception: his words about the Last Judgment (Mathew 25: 31-46) are often read on a literal level only. That's the passage about providing food and water and clothing to the least of his people. For centuries, Catholics have learned and perhaps memorized the list of "corporal works of mercy," seven specific services that we might provide when we are trying to deepen a Christian life with more prayer and fasting and almsgiving. Six of the seven are taken from Matthew's Gospel; the seventh is from the Book of Tobit. We read the passage literally, and St. James pounds on the importance of concrete (literal) services: good so far. We usually read the passage literally *only*: this is bizarre, and crippling.

When you read the passage on many levels, the same way we read the rest of Scripture, it turns out to be as complex and as fascinating as the rest of the words of Jesus. The passage is not a handful of random examples of service; it's a structured list, with three pairs, each pair alternating between a call to imitate the Lord and a call to give to the Lord. All six precepts should be understood on many levels; but the first pair is primarily about the needs of the body, and the second pair is primarily about the needs of the soul, and the third is primarily about the needs of the spirit. The traditional list of "corporal works" scrambles the order, so you can't see the orderly progression.

Studying the works of mercy as presented in the Gospel makes the social nature of all these acts clear. It is possible to give alms privately, but it is not possible to welcome someone into a community without a community. The Lord's command to "welcome strangers" is actually more like "sweep outsiders into your gathering."

When you read the list of merciful acts as Matthew presents it, it seems to me that the sixth work of mercy provides a solid foundation for the Social Gospel. Instead of seeing people who do wrong as sinners – as spiritual criminals – the Lord seems to see us as people who are trapped. So he's not focusing on how to punish us justly; he's focused on how to set us free. He's not the judge or jailer; he's the savior. This approach makes it much easier to understand the importance of sins of omission – the things we fail to do that would have been good. This approach does not focus on who wronged whom, but rather on how we will help each other out of the mess. It's not focused on past evils, but on future goods.

Restoring the Works of Mercy is available from Amazon ($8.50) or Kindle ($3).

#50: Conclusion

So what do I want you to understand, to accept, to do?

I'm a pro-lifer, and I'm a Democrat. This is not a contradiction; I am where I belong.

Democrats and Republicans can and should provide a mechanism for balancing competing rights and responsibilities, for competing visions of the future, for competing approaches to all civic questions. We're not enemies, I would hope; and for sure, we're not supposed to be.

The pro-life movement is badly crippled when it tries to move forward without the perspective of pro-life Democrats. The movement needs, among other things:

- a respect for wisdom, especially the teaching from Jesus in his Sermon on the Mount;
- a commitment to nonviolence, which is incompatible with the habit of demonizing our opponents;
- a clear understanding of social sin, which isn't a partisan concept at all, but is used far more often by Democrats than by Republicans;
- a feminist approach, especially since protecting a child depends on enlisting his mother's help;
- working alliances or coalitions or workable and amiable relationships with other movements fighting for peace and justice;
- and a vision that embraces all America, all Americans – *and also* all people of good will throughout the world.

On the night before he died, Jesus of Nazareth prayed for his followers: Father, may they all be one, as you and I are one.

Amen? Amen!

About the Author

John Cavanaugh-O'Keefe is best known for his work as an activist, building the nonviolent branch of the pro-life movement. He has been called by "Father of the Rescue movement" by *Time*, *NY Times Magazine*, Joan Andrews, Joe Scheidler, and others. *LA Times* writer Jim Risen's history of the rescue movement, *Wrath of Angels*, also uses this title. Cavanaugh-O'Keefe notes that the title is odd, because the real leaders of the rescue movement were mostly women, including Jeanne Miller Gaetano, Dr. Lucy Hancock, Jo McGowan, Joan Andrews, Juli Loesch Wiley, Kathie O'Keefe, ChristyAnne Collins, Monica Migliorino Miller, and many others. Nonetheless, his writing – especially *No Cheap Solutions* and *Emmanuel, Solidarity: God's Act, Our Response* – influenced activists in the US, Canada, Mexico, Brazil, all over Europe, Philippines, Korea, and Australia.

Cavanaugh-O'Keefe has been arrested 39 times for civil disobedience. He was in the first group that was jailed for pro-life nonviolent action (in Connecticut, 1978). He was among the three organizers of the "We Will Stand Up" campaign, the most successful event of the rescue movement, closing all the abortion clinics in eight of the nine cities that Pope John Paul II visited in 1987. He initiated the Tobit Project, taking bodies out of dumpsters in the Washington area and providing respectful burials.

He has written extensively about eugenics and population control; see especially *The Roots of Racism and Abortion*. He participated in efforts to resist the population reduction campaigns, particularly in South Africa under the apartheid government, and in Bangladesh; see especially "Deadly Neocolonialism." He supported the work of the Information Project for Africa, which brought feminists and pro-lifers together to resist coercive depopulation measures at the UN population conference in Cairo.

He has written about eugenics and human cloning. When President Clinton established his National Bioethics Advisory Commission (NBAC), Cavanaugh-O'Keefe helped form a grass-roots commission in response – the American Bioethics Advisory Commission (ABAC), and served as the ABAC's first executive director. The first policy question that the Clinton's NBAC addressed was human cloning, and their report has sections on eugenics and dignity that were written in response to input from Cavanaugh-O'Keefe. When the NBAC published their report supporting human cloning as long as the clone is destroyed in the embryonic or fetal stage, the ABAC worked with the United States Conference of Catholic Bishops against this "clone-and-kill" proposal.

Throughout his life, Cavanaugh-O'Keefe has worked to cross-fertilize, and to maintain civil dialogue with opponents. He worked with Prolifers for Survival, as editor of the group's publication, *P.S.* This ambitious organization brought peace activists and pro-life activists together; their challenging work was later taken over by Cardinal Bernardin. Cavanaugh-O'Keefe was proud to be invited to contribute to the *Women's Studies Encyclopedia*, to write their article explaining the pro-life movement. He worked with a common ground group in the Washington area, bringing pro-life and pro-choice activists together – not to find compromises, but to encourage respect and understanding.

In 2012, Cavanaugh-O'Keefe began working toward a consistent ethic of hospitality, strengthening the unity of the Catholic Church by encouraging pro-life and pro-family activists to re-consider their positions on immigration, and encouraging pro-immigration activists to reconsider their positions on life and marriage. See www.SignoftheCrossing.org.

He and his wife live in Maryland, where they raised six children and now enjoy 15 (plus) grandchildren.

Sign of the Crossing
6510 Damascus Rd
Laytonsville, MD 20882